Creative Holiday Learning Year 6

Timothy Tuck

PASCAL PRESS

Brief Contents

Contents

Contents (cont)

Contents (cont)

MUSIC

Contents (cont)

Contents (cont)

Contents (cont)

Contents (cont)

Contents (cont)

Contents (cont)

Lights, Camera, Action!

Welcome to GMG Productions, the home of Great Movie Gems!

It is wonderful to see you all here today and we hope you're going to have a great time touring the GMG movie lot, visiting our special film school and experiencing first hand the excitement that is movie making.

We're going to be visiting six different film sets absolutely adrift in a sea of puzzles but along the way you're going to meet some exclusive GMG features, so here is a quick guide to the more common ones.

Genre Busters

Most movies fit into set genres or categories, such as comedy, action or fantasy. Genre busters give you more information about films in each category.

Movie Posters

Don't rush past the movie posters; you'll need to look at them carefully to solve the poster-poser puzzles.

Trivia

Not puzzles, just little snippets of information about films in each genre.

Storyboards

Each movie has a set of ten storyboards. Each storyboard has part of the movie's story, a still from the movie and a puzzle.

Directors' Bios

There are plenty of famous directors out there in movieland but unfortunately none of them work for GMG. So we've included the biographies of a few real directors. But you've got to work out who they are. Sorry.

Hollywood Crossquizzes

Special puzzles made up of the pairs of letters in the word HOLLYWOOD.

Movie Matrix

Special puzzles made with the word MOVIE in them. Oh, and a hidden answer too.

What Is My Job?

Solve the puzzle and learn more about a few of the occupations found on the movie set.

Film School

These are brief excursions into different aspects of movie making. Find out about film shots, movie theatres, rating systems and more.

Project

A special open-ended activity involving watching films or thinking creatively. Or both.

Learning More

Internet links for more information on the directors, films and activities in each chapter.

Now... any questions?

No, you don't have to complete the puzzles in order, though the storyboards will make more sense that way. You might find some of the questions test your ingenuity but don't give up. You can pat yourself on the back when you've worked them out. Then go and test Mum or Dad and impress them with how clever you are!

No, none of these films are real. But if you'd like to take an option on any of the ideas, please contact the author.

No, there are no toilets on the bus.
Please go BEFORE we leave. Thank you.

Right. Enough talk, let's hop on board the bus and be off…

Out and About the Lot

The tour bus leaves the GMG office (START) and visits six movie sets. It never travels over the same section of road twice and it eventually leaves via the exit.

1. Which six sets do the tour group get to see? Tick their boxes.

2. Each set has a circled number. Find that letter in the genre title and write it, **in order visited***, in the space below. Now you know what the studio intends to do with movies the bus **didn't** visit:

___ ___ ___ ___ ___ ___ **them.**

*And no, it's not the same order as the chapters in the book.

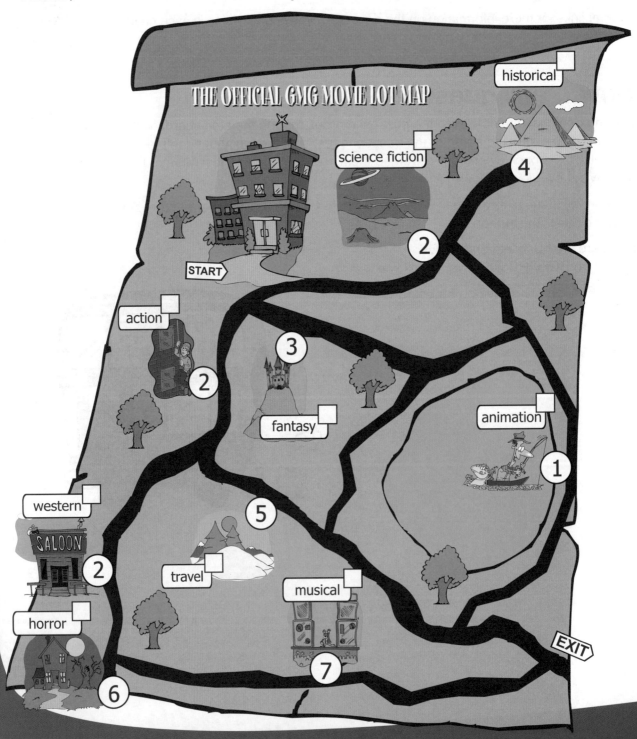

The Journey Begins...

Starbeamers III

Starbeamers III is the third episode in GMG Films' highly successful science fiction series starring kleptomaniacal aliens who steal people, places and low-cal soft drinks.

Security on the filmset is tight as the studio doesn't want any pre-release details to escape. If all goes to plan, there'll eventually be over a dozen Starbeamer films.

But which one of these projected titles has been misspelt?

Starbeamers VII: Lost and Found

Starbeamers VIIII: Missing In Action

Starbeamers IX: Beam Me Down

Starbeamers X: The Bulb's Blown

Genre Buster

Science Fiction films are a type of fantasy film. They are often set in the future and usually feature space travel, advanced technology, alien beings and have lavish special effects. They infrequently feature penguins in space suits.

Gross Science Fiction Films

Here's a list of 10 of the highest grossing (money earning) science fiction films of all time.* The titles are just a little bit mixed up though. Your mission, should you choose to accept it: fix 'em up!

Instructions

1. Read the last word in each film title.

2. Match it to its correct first word (or phrase).

3. Write in the matching word and year in the spaces provided.

Tip: Cross out each word as you use it. (See the example on the grid.)

* Figures were correct at the time of writing.

Box Office Gross	Film Title		Year	
$563,000,000	Jurassic Apes		2001	
$505,000,000	Independence Wars		1977	
$491,314,983	Star Wars: Episode I — Phantom Park		1993	
$337,600,000	Star Wars: Episode II — Attack of the Jedi		1983	
$337,100,000	Men in Future		1985	
$337,000,000	Star Menace		1999	
$263,700,000	Star Wars: Episode VI — Return of the Clones		2002	
$200,100,000	Fifth Day		1996	
$178,900,000	Planet of the ~~Element~~	*Apes*	1998	*2001*
$140,000,000	Back to the Black		1997	

Science Fiction

Posters Posers

All the answers to these puzzles are on the poster.

Anagrammaticals

The poster lists four stars. Unjumble their names to make anagrams that mean:

1. PASH SPICE

Vehicle propelled by a rocket.

s p a c e _ s h i p

2. VINE USER

Everything, everywhere.

u n i v e r s e

3. KAHL COBLE

A collapsed star that 'sucks' in light and gravity.

B l a c k _ h o l e

4. ACE POSTURE

Space outside the Earth's atmosphere.

O _ _ _ _ _ _ _ _ _ _

Quick Numbers

Find 3 different ways that '3' has been displayed on the poster.

1. The alien's fingers
2. The third episode
3. They came, they saw, they....mum. Used in words

Word Trivia

'Folderol' is an old word that means 'silly nonsense'.

Synopsis Search

Now you find the answer to the burning question:

What did the alien say to his friend wearing a Greek jug on his head?

Instructions

1. Read the succinct and exciting synopsis of the new *Starbeamers*© *III* movie.

2. Search for each word (of four letters or more) and (this is the important bit) cross them out.

3. When you finish you'll have a goodly number of letters left over — 29 to be exact. Write these lonely letters (in order from left to right) into the spaces below.

4. Have a good chuckle at the wacky alien humour.

__ __ __ __   __ __ __ __ __,   __ __ __ __ __ __ __   __ __ __ __   __ __ __ __

__ __ __ __ __ __   __ __ __ __ __?

'The inhabitants of Earth awake one morning to find their most precious world famous landmarks stolen by the infamous Starbeamer aliens. With intergalactic agent Tan Metal and the TELMANAT team in hot pursuit aboard the Star Rats spaceship the safe return of the world's treasures seems assured. But can the lone Terran ship survive the fearsome fire power of the aliens' battle fleet? And why do the aliens actually want the Sydney Opera House?'

```
H E Y W H A T S D S S A T U R R N S T A R B E A M E R D
O I N G O T L N R Y O M A I U R H E A E F A S D M A E T
S Z K F K S O T A K N D E L S U R V I V E W E L T T A B
R T I B Q O N F O M Z H L E I Y G N F L D H N D C R S P
Z R A W E M E K B L T K D R S E C B Y E S A C P D H U U
E W I R P S T F A Q A P X Z O S N M R T A T Z I W N O R
D L X V R R U A A G E N T H D W R S N E X R K H W N M S
L N R Q Q A E O N D L M D L B L W A F J V P S S L A A U
N P O W E R T C H A M K R M M L T M I G L O N O S R F I
H D M C W T N S I D M O P J A I L P N K N B C E M R N T
T P B T E E L F V O W L Y L B R I R D H A I R S R E I P
R B W B K H P J B M U L E A F H K H Y Y S U N E I T Q D
A P L A T E M M S M L S H T S K K S T M S J T R M D P S
E Q F H T I W Y Y A K N A E A V Q R E A U U L N O N D T
F A M O U S D Q U W I W C R Q K V A E T R H W L D M W O
F K L M N N W T M K A A E L T K N R K N E V L A L J R L
H B Q N E V C T D K P P N T L S T N K P D R W X N H W E
W N M Y L A H V E S O C I N T E R G A L A C T I C T W N
```

Science Fiction

3D Navigation

Navigation through space isn't easy; there's at least three dimensions to consider…(and don't even think about time travel!).

To get an idea of how tricky it is, try following the flight path below. Write down the order you reach each planet.

1. Start at A1-1 (square A1 on level 1) and fly to A1-5 (A1 on level 5).

2. Connect the two squares with a straight line. Which planet do you pass through? Write a '1' in its box.

3. Repeat for the other pairs of coordinates in turn.

A1-1 » A1-5

A1-5 » D1-5

D1-5 » A1-2

A1-2 » D4-5

D4-5 » D4-1

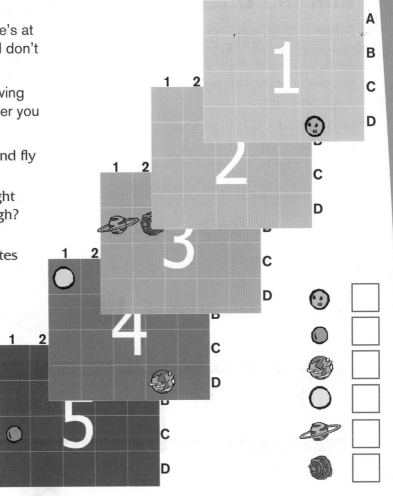

SF Film Trivia

A Trip to the Moon (1902) was probably the first SF film.

STORYBOARD 1

`Midnight on a warm January evening at the abandoned fairground.`
`The menacing alien spacecraft appears from beneath the grass.`

Picture Puzzle

Each of the Ferris Wheel's eight carriages are painted with a number in a simple pattern. What number is on the hidden carriage at the bottom? Look for a clue in the storyboard description. Hopefully, it won't take a MONTH of Sundays to work out.

Jumbled Director

Starbeamers III was directed by the not-so-famous director GREA GLUCOSE. But if you rearrange the stills from the movie strip below, you'll discover the name of a much better known director.

To help you, the sequence starts with the bullhorn held high and ends with it held low. You could also try to work the director's name out by reading his biography opposite.

___ ___ ___ ___ ___ ___

___ ___ ___ ___ ___ ___

Director Bio

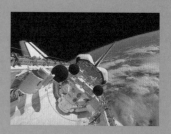

I was raised in the USA on a walnut ranch. My first big film was *American Graffiti* which I followed with *Star Wars* four years later. I helped produce the *Indiana Jones* series, founded the special effects company called Industrial Light and Magic and LucasArts, a computer game company. My *Star Wars* episodes are all amongst the highest grossing films of all time.

G   R   E   A

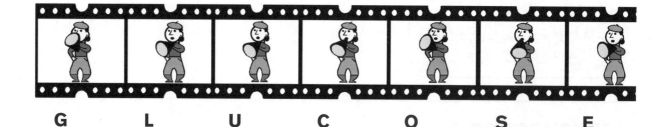

G   L   U   C   O   S   E

STORYBOARD 2

Green lights flash as the alien commander activates the spacecraft's anti-detection screens.

Picture Puzzle

The alien is thinking out aloud—unfortunately in alien! To help you translate the word, each different symbol stands for a different letter of the word. Look for a clue in the picture.

Science Fiction

Hollywood Crossquiz

Ah, the lure of the lights of Hollywood! In this crossquiz unfortunately only the 'LL' lights are on. Use the clues to complete the rest of the squares.

printed sheet of paper advertising a show

from the beginning

in the nearby area

soft song sung to a baby

loud shout

leather folded case for money

protective clothing for workers

sell more than anybody else

moving trolley for film cameras

H
O L L
O L L
L U L L a b y
Y e L L
W a L L e t
O v e r a L L s
O L L
D O L L y

STORYBOARD 3

Under a night sky, a luckless camper is sucked into the spaceship.

Picture Puzzle

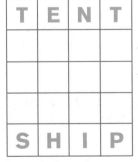

T	E	N	T
S	H	I	P

caused something to go

writing instruments

pointed metal sticks

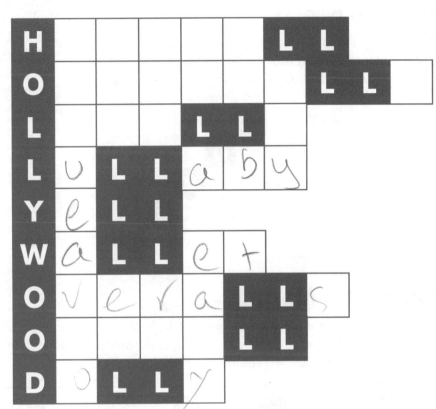

Change a TENT into a SHIP by changing just one letter on each new line. You may change the order of the letters to create each new word.

Science Fiction

Movie Matrix

Use the clues and the given letter to complete the movie matrix. When completed, one of the columns will answer this question:

What Are We?

Human-like, these small, supernatural troublemakers have featured in many stories. They also bear a passing likeness to many movie aliens!

	M				
encounters →		O			
toy doll →			V		
underground caverns →				I	
belonging to them →	n	e	r	v	E
sense connected with the tongue →					

SF Film Trivia

The 1950s saw Earth being invaded regularly: by crustaceans in *Attack of the Crab Monsters* (1957), by freshwater worms in *Attack of the Giant Leeches* (1959), carnivorous dinosaurs from the deep in *The Beast from 20,000 Fathoms* (1953), and gigantic mutant ants in *Them!* (1954).

Make-up Magic

Di Gussie (the actor playing the alien in *Starbeamers III*®) is a STAR who's played many different roles in many different movies. But she's usually wearing so much make-up nobody can recognise her. See if you can; just one of the actors below isn't Di.

Di Gussie — Star   **A**   **B**   **C**   **D**   **E**   **F**

STORYBOARD 4

The next 'pick-up' is a trailer full of Vegemite® from a lonely Australian highway.

Picture Puzzle

The trailer has a volume of 240 m³. What are the dimensions of the ends of the trailer?

(a)   8m × 6m

(b)   4m × 3m

(c)   5m × 6m

Science Fiction

Movie Match-up

Which 1979 science fiction film had the tagline 'In space no one can hear you scream?'

To find out (or just to check your answer):

1. Find the three-letter mini-words hiding in these longer words.

2. Connect (using straight lines) the two words whose mini-words are anagrams of each other.

3. Write down the letters the lines cross through.

4. Unjumble the letters to create the film's name.

The first one is done for you.

a _ _ e _

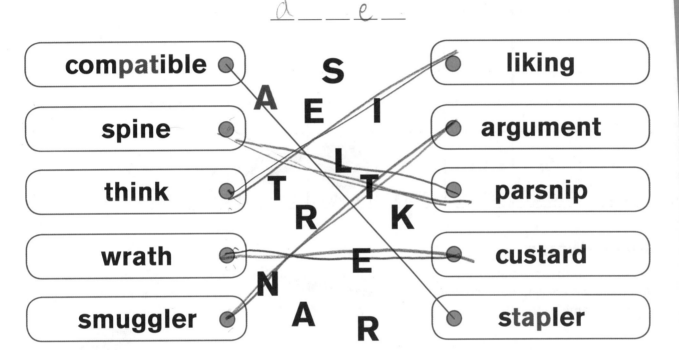

compatible · · liking

spine · · argument

think · · parsnip

wrath · · custard

smuggler · · stapler

A S E I L T R K N E A R

STORYBOARD 5

Oh no! Now the aliens are abducting the Earth's important landmarks! High over Paris flies the famous Eiffel Tower!

Picture Puzzle

The Eiffel Tower weighs 10,100 tonnes and is joined together with, well, a lot of rivets.
To work out how many, count the number of French flags fluttering in the photo and multiply by, say, 100,000.

9

Planet Shuffle

Arrghh! The Starbeamers have rearranged the solar system—into order by planetary diameter! Please fix this mess up (in less than six moves) by shifting just one planet at a time and allowing the other planets to move up. There are a few different ways to do it!

Jupiter	Saturn	Uranus	Neptune	Earth	Venus	Mars	Mercury	Pluto
Mercury	Venus	Earth	Mars	Jupiter	Saturn	Uranus	Neptune	Pluto

Planet Words

Now the Starbeamers are showing off their advanced vocabulary. Perhaps they're entered into an Intergalactic spelling bee! So what are the words they've spelt out from the initial letter of each planet's name?

1. ____

2. ____

3. ____

4. ____

STORYBOARD 6

It's the Statue of Liberty's turn to be starbeamed into space.

Picture Puzzle

Which three numbers on the bottom of the spacecraft add up to the Statue of Liberty's full height of 93 m?

Base (smallest) _____   Pedestal _____

Statue (largest) _____

10

Science Fiction

ARFS*

Ace Posture, Pash Spice and Vine User are the three principal stars of *Starbeamers III*. Use the information given below to complete the table detailing the actors' roles, their salaries and the number of films they've appeared in.

1. The hero makes the least money.

2. Pash has been in the most films.

3. Ace would like to play a scientist one day.

4. The camper makes more money than Ace but less than Pash.

5. The actor on $300,000 negotiated a pay rise for the second film.

* Actor, role, film and salary. Also Absolutely Ridiculous Footnotes.

		ROLE			FILM			SALARY		
		camper	hero	scientist	one film	two films	three films	$100,000	$300,000	$2,500,000
ACTOR	Ace Posture									
	Pash Spice									
	Vine User									
SALARY	$100,000									
	$300,000									
	$2,500,000									
FILMS	one film									
	two films									
	three films									

ACTOR	ROLE	FILMS	SALARY

STORYBOARD 7

Lost! The aliens stop to ask for directions to their next landmark.

Picture Puzzle

The aliens are told (nicely) to go one kilometre:

north, west, east, south, east, north, west, south, west, north and finally east.

Are they now north, south, east or west of where they started?

Spiral Galaxy

Surviving in the hostile environment of outer space is about making the right decisions at the right time. Do you press the red button or the green button? Do you blast the red monster in front of you or the green one behind you? Do you fly into the spiral galaxy in the red spacecraft or the green one? The choice is yours—but the answers are the same. Write the letters of the answers into the stars. The first one is done for you. If you get stuck, just attack the problem from the other end!

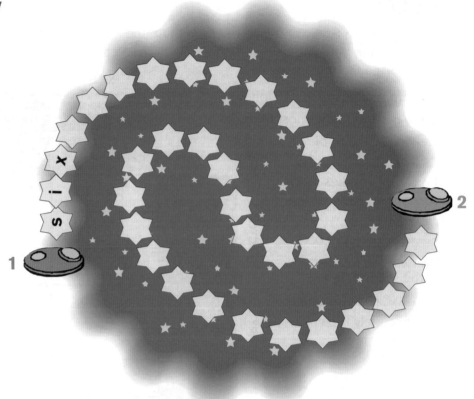

Spacecraft 1 Clues

a. Number of planets further from the sun than Earth. (3)

b. Book of maps. (5)

c. Disease-carrying rodents. (4)

d. Not even once. (5)

e. Snakelike aquatic animal. (3)

f. _____ pong. (4)

g. Steal. (3)

h. King of the beasts (4)

i. Loud argument. (3)

Spacecraft 2 Clues

a. Damaged by long use. (4)

b. Greasy liquid. (3)

c. Clone-like alien race from Star Trek. (4)

d. Quick bite. (3)

e. Unpleasant smile. (4)

f. Not odd. (4)

g. Distant sun. (4)

h. White crystals used in cooking. (4)

i. Line about which a planet rotates. (4)

STORYBOARD 8

The Sydney Opera House sails over the harbour, destination unknown.

Picture Puzzle

A huge hole has been torn in the roof of the building. How many tiles are missing?

Science Fiction

What's My Job?

Rearrange the letters below to spell out this job title. Use the green square letter 4 times and the yellow square letter twice.

I'm a member of the sound crew. My job is to hold a microphone attached to a long pole. I hold this above the actors' heads as they speak.

P	O	M
E		B
A	R	T

_____ _____ _____

Spot the Silhouette

Ace Posture is racing after the spacecraft that has captured Pash Spice, the scientist. He can see a computer-enhanced image on the com-screen but is faced with a problem. Which of the seven silhouetted spacecraft is the matching one?

SF Film Trivia

The Millennium Falcon spacecraft in *Star Wars* (1977) was inspired by a hamburger bun.

STORYBOARD 9

```
Loaded down with their loot,
the spacecraft head home
past Jupiter.
```

Picture Puzzle

What's the missing letter in this sequence?

M · V · E · M · ___ · S · U · N · P

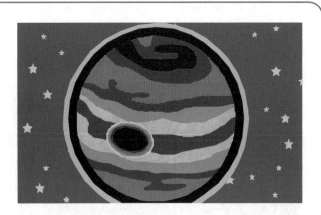

The Final Countdown

Meanwhile, back on Earth, a rescue mission has been assembled. The spacecraft is on the launch pad and the countdown has begun. It's not quite the usual countdown though. Please rescue the rescuers by supplying (in the correct order of course) the final three numbers.

What's Next?

Hopefully you won't have to dive 20,000 leagues under the sea, travel from the Earth to the moon or journey to the centre of the Earth to find the missing letter.

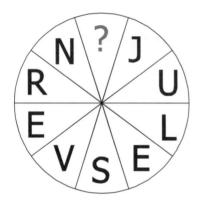

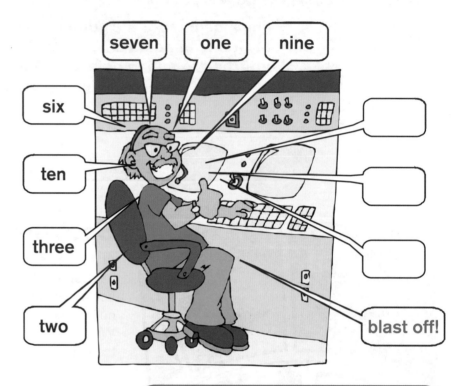

seven · one · nine

six

ten

three

two

blast off!

SF Film Trivia

The DeLorean car time-machine in *Back to the Future* (1985) was originally planned to be a refrigerator.

STORYBOARD 10

The Starbeamers interrogate their Earthly captive.

Picture Puzzle

What has changed between these two frames of the film? (There are 10 differences.)

Science Fiction

From S to F

Discovering an abandoned spacecraft on planet S (for 'Starbeamers') the kidnapped humans make a run for planet F (for 'Freedom'. Or more likely, 'Fast Food'). In fact, they make ten runs, each one along an orbital path. To stave off boredom they write a gigantic letter on each passing moon, to complete the five-letter words described by the clues. When they finish they discover to their amazement that the letters on the red moons spell out (in clockwise order) the first word in the title of the Science Fiction film: 'AI'.

PS Some of these are quite tricky. See the word list below and perhaps use a dictionary to help out.

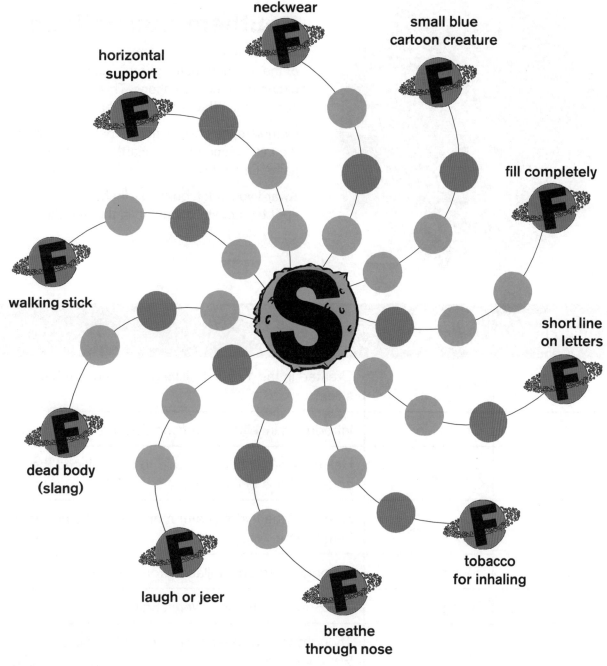

neckwear

small blue cartoon creature

horizontal support

fill completely

walking stick

short line on letters

dead body (slang)

tobacco for inhaling

laugh or jeer

breathe through nose

Word list

scarf, scoff, serif, shelf, smurf, sniff, snuff, staff, stiff, stuff

Constellations

In ancient times, stargazers imagined close groups of stars to be connected and mentally 'joined-the-dots' to create pictures.

Twelve of these constellations are now more often remembered for their connection with people's star-signs.

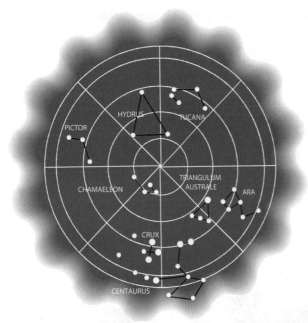

Southern Constellations

This star map shows a few of the constellations of the southern hemisphere. These are all circumpolar constellations. This means they can be seen throughout the year.

Complete the chart of names below by matching the Latin name (on the chart) with the common name (in the table).

Award yourself a gold star (hah!) if you can spot the constellations up in the real sky.

Latin Name	Common Name	
	Painter's Easel	Created in the 1750s to fill a gap in the southern skies!
	Chameleon	Introduced in 1603 by Johann Bayer for a sky atlas.
	Centaur	Half human/half horse. Is said to have placed the constellations in the sky.
	Water snake	A twin for the hydra (water monster) of the northern hemisphere.
	Toucan	A tropical bird constellation from Johann Bayer.
	Triangle	The Southern Triangle. Very original!
	Southern Cross	Thought to have been visible in the Middle East 2000 years ago!
	Altar	Suggests the altars that the Greeks and Romans used for sacrifices.

Zodiac Match-up

How good a stargazer would you make? Below are the 12 star-sign constellations.
Use the pictures to help you label each one correctly.

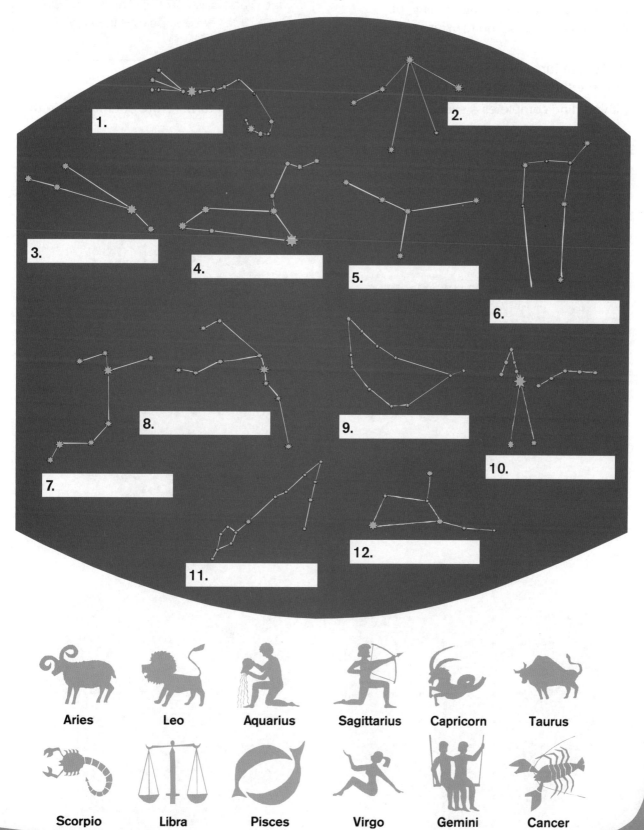

1. _____

2. _____

3. _____

4. _____

5. _____

6. _____

7. _____

8. _____

9. _____

10. _____

11. _____

12. _____

Aries **Leo** **Aquarius** **Sagittarius** **Capricorn** **Taurus**

Scorpio **Libra** **Pisces** **Virgo** **Gemini** **Cancer**

Science Fiction

Fences

Ah, the universe can be such a lonely place…
so take a break from being Han Solo and try
beating your best friend with a game of
Intergalactic Fences. The rules are simple:

SF Film Trivia

The actors playing C-3PO and R2-D2 in
*Star Wars: Episode III–Revenge of the
Sith* (2005) have appeared in every *Star
Wars* film.

1. Take it in turns to connect two adjacent
   dots, either horizontally or vertically.

2. If your line completes a square you win one point and an extra turn. (Write your initials in the
   square to remember who won it.)

3. You win bonuses if you fence a planet (2 points) or a star (3 points).

4. The game ends when all pairs of dots have been connected. The winner, naturally enough,
   is the person with the most points.

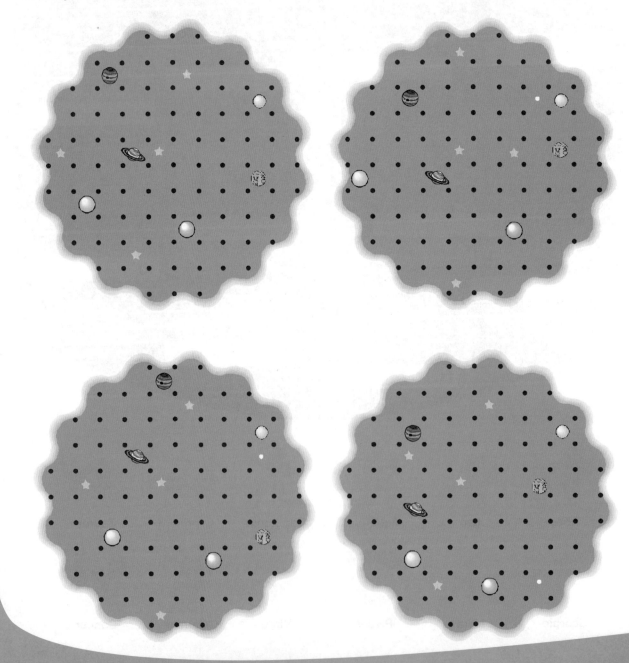

Science Fiction

The Starbeamers III® Trivia Quiz

How much attention were you paying to the *Starbeamers III®* storyboard pictures? Not much you say? Well, silly you. Now you're faced with a quiz and there's nothing you can do about it! (Technically of course you could just not do the quiz, you could cheat and look at the pictures again or just copy the answers from the back of the book. But hypothetically let's say you're not going to do that and you're really going to try your very, very best. Good onya!)

Instructions

You really need them? Okay… first read the question about each storyboard picture, then circle the best answer. Got all that?

1. When the spacecraft bursts from the ground at the fairground which of these objects isn't in the picture?
   (**a**) roller coaster
   (**b**) ferris wheel
   (**c**) dodgem cars
   (**d**) circus tent

2. Is the aliens's space helmet:
   (**a**) green
   (**b**) red
   (**c**) blue
   (**d**) silver

3. Is the campsite near:
   (**a**) the sea
   (**b**) a river
   (**c**) mountains
   (**d**) a road

4. How many vehicles are on the road with the semi-trailer?
   (**a**) 0
   (**b**) 1
   (**c**) 2
   (**d**) 3

5. What else was starbeamed with the Eiffel Tower?
   (**a**) a French cafe
   (**b**) a bird
   (**c**) a train
   (**d**) the ground

6. Which American landmark was starbeamed?
   (**a**) the Statue of Liberty
   (**b**) Mount Rushmore
   (**c**) the White House
   (**d**) the Golden Gate Bridge

7. What food was advertised outside the restaurant where the aliens stopped to ask directions?
   (**a**) steak sandwiches
   (**b**) tacos
   (**c**) pizzas
   (**d**) hamburgers

8. Which country was the Opera House starbeamed from?
   (**a**) Germany
   (**b**) England
   (**c**) France
   (**d**) Australia

9. What was the most significant feature of the planet?
   (**a**) huge rings
   (**b**) huge spot
   (**c**) huge moons
   (**d**) a huge mountain

10. The starbeamer alien was interrogating a:
    (**a**) pig
    (**b**) koala
    (**c**) raccoon
    (**d**) dog

Learning More

FILMS

Official *Star Wars* website
www.starwars.com

Science Fiction Films
www.scifi.com

George Lucas
www.george.lucas.net

SPACE

Exploring the Planets
www.nasm.si.edu/etp

Constellations: Windows to the Universe
www.windows.ucar.edu

AUTHORS

Jules Verne
www.kirjasto.sci.fi/verne.htm

PLACES

The Eiffel Tower
www.tour-eiffel.fr

Statue of Liberty
www.nps.gov/stli

Sydney Opera House
www.sydneyoperahouse.com

I've Been Framed!

Wide shot? Close-up? Extreme close-up? Choosing how much (or how little) of a scene is an important decision for the director. Here are six basic camera shots:

1. **Extreme Wide Shot (EWS)**
   This shot sets a scene. You can't see the subjects but you can see their surroundings.

2. **Wide Shot (WS)**
   Here are the subjects—and we can see them from their heads to (almost) their toes.

3. **Medium Shot (MS)**
   Closer and more detail. We just can't see their feet.

4. **Medium Close-up (MCU)**
   The subjects' faces are clearer—but we're not too close.

5. **Close-up (CU)**
   The faces now take up most of the screen.

6. **Extreme Close-up (ECU)**
   Up close and personal. Check out that smile!

What's the Shot?

Below are six frames from a ballooning film. Use the camera shot information to classifiy them as EWS, WS, MS, MCU, CU or ECU. The shaded letters will spell out the title of a popular tourist attraction.

FILM SCHOOL

film shots

Shoot for the Moon

The director has asked for some special shots in the latest films.

Use the description in the synopsis to identify each of the pictured film shots.

Synopsis:

We'll start with a **dramatic angle** shot of the enemy's headquarters. Then cut to the top of the tower: I want an **object POV** showing just the city and binoculars. Then change to a **mask vignette** that shows the watcher's view through the glasses.

Big cut now; a **split screen** showing the two agents talking to each other.

Give me a **tilted horizon** as the mother walks by—it'll add to the tension.

When we see the ranger I want a strong **silhouette** shot followed by a **reflection** shot of the pub. Then we're back to the main story; add a **sub-clip** to show what's happening back at mission control.

PROJECT

Camera Shot Watch

Watch 5 minutes of your favourite movie. Make a tally of the camera shots you see.

Movie Title

1. Extreme Wide Shot (EWS)
2. Wide Shot (WS)
3. Medium Shot (MS)

4. Medium Close-up (MCU)
5. Close-up (CU)
6. Extreme Close-up (ECU)

What other special shots do you see?

1. Reflection
2. Split scene
3. Sub-clip

4. Tilted horizon
5. Object POV
6. Masked vignette

7. Silhouette
8. Dramatic angle

Hardly Working

Hardly Working is GMG Productions' movie length version of its popular cartoon series featuring the bumbling, accident-prone serial-careerist, Hardly M Ployed.

Hardly Original

Of course, the original Hardly cartoons were pretty basic. Simply drawn, coloured and photographed original Hardly Working sketches are nonetheless worth big money. So which of these four drawings is an original?

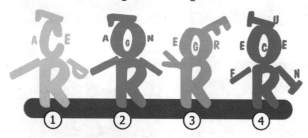

Genre Buster

Animated films use a series of individual pictures that each differs slightly from the one before, giving an illusion of movement. Early animators simply photographed hand-drawn pictures. Modern animation techniques include computer-generated 3D images. Although animated films appeal to children you could say that animation is really a film production technique rather than a genre.

Hardly Rhyming

Each of the first season's episodes of *Hardly Working* began with an educational riddle that described Hardly's latest job. For a nostalgic trip down memory lane, here's the riddle from Episode 1:

My first is in BET but isn't in JET   ____

My second's in LOG and also in LET   ____

My third's not in ROT but sure is in RAT   ____

My fourth's not in BAT but is there in CAT   ____

My fifth is in SKI but isn't in SIT   ____

My sixth is in SIT but nowhere in BIT   ____

My seventh's in MARS but isn't in SOAR   ____

My eighth is in FIRE but, nope, not in FORE   ____

My ninth is in PAST but isn't in PASH   ____

My last is in LASH but not found in LAST   ____

Stop horsing around!

Neigh!

Hardly Working (1921)

My whole is a job that needs lots of heat, for putting iron shoes on big smelly feet.

Animation

Poster Posers

All the answers to these puzzles are on the poster.

Anagrammaticals

The poster lists five stars who provided the voices for the movie. Each is actually an anagram of one of Hardly's (many) career paths. Use the clues and the poster to help!

1. CO TROD diagnoses illnesses and cares for the sick.

— — — — — — —

2. CHORT SHOELACE supervises students and helps them learn.

— — — — — — —

— — — — — — —

3. DES TINT is an oral surgeon.

— — — — — — —

4. SASH DERRIRE cuts, washes and trims curls and tresses.

— — — — — — — — — — —

5. JACK RUMBLE also cuts, but doesn't usually wash or trim his trees before he fells them.

— — — — — — — — — —

Quick Count

How many words beginning with HAR can you find on the poster?

Word Trivia

Our word **episode** comes from the Greek word **epeisodion** which means 'addition'.

Blank Cheques

Accountant Cathie Jones has signed these cheques in readiness for paying the eccentric head animator Robert L Jackson. But before they're filled (and cashed) in… look at the cheques, and as far as you can see:

Which cheque is on top? _____

Which two cheques are identical? _____ and _____

Which cheque is at the bottom? _____

Which cheque number is missing? _____

Which cheque has the name spelt incorrectly? _____

But now for the fun part. LFL Productions (a subsidiary of GMG) owes Robert L Jackson the grand total of $12,345. Cathie's made out one cheque already (J) for $3.00. Fill in the remaining cheques with **eight different** amounts **using only the number 5**. You may use a zero to complete the tens or units of the cents amount.

Hint: Write down as many amounts as you can think of with only 5s in them, such as $55 or $555.50.

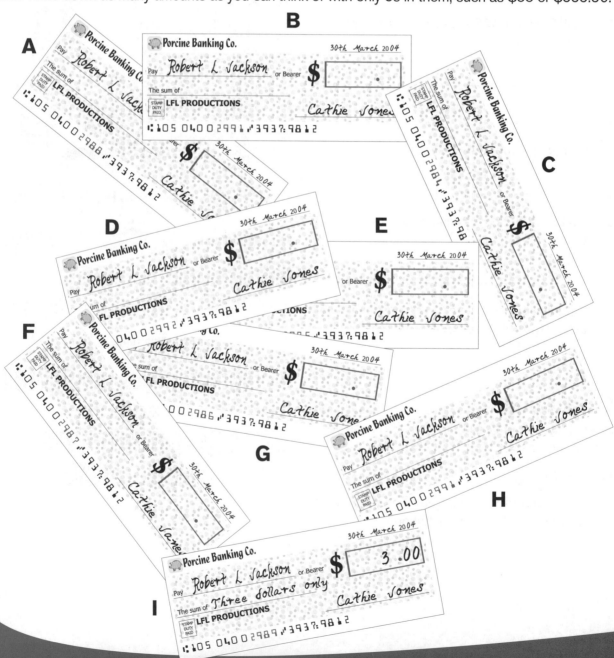

Animation

Synopsis Search

What did Hardly say to his wife when she asked him **'How's your job at the lemon factory?'**

Instructions

1. Read the short synopsis then cross out each word (of four letters or more).

2. When you finish write the first 34 leftover letters in the spaces below.

___ ___ ___ ___ ___ ___ ___ ___ ___ , ___ ___ , ___ ___ ___ ___ ___ ___ ___ ___

___ ___ ___ ___ ___ ___ ___ ___ ___ ___ ___ ___ ___ ___

___ ___ ___

This animated movie tells the story of the world's most experienced (and least successful) job seeker. After years of serial-sackings things begin to look up for the Ployed family when the international employment agency 'Jobs-R-Us' takes Hardly on as a publicity stunt. Trial assignments (including crop duster, parachute instructor and construction worker) almost end in disaster but company boss Mr Hardegree finally places our foolhardy hero in the National Idiom Testing laboratory where his inexpert, clumsy incompetence is just what the scientists ordered. Then the twins Harrison and Harrietta uncover an unscrupulous secret corporate plot…

```
H A R T R I A L M O V I E R R T S U J N O S I R R A H I E
T I U E V E Y H A D B I N C O M P E T E N C E I T D S G S
E T N E K R J S T N E M Y O L P M E S T U N T O U R N D R
R B C S L E T H M A N N E H W S T H T E R C E S A I L I E
E K O U A D E S O U N E W D C C O R P O R A T E D R L J T
H O V N I Q E S T T L H K I J P P Q C D T E Y U O R G I F
W O E S R H W C S A A C E S V N N X W R R Y L W P R Y N A
V L R C E A B O N T K N D A K O A J T D O C T N N C M T F
R I W R S R M H P E T E S S I H O T E W N P M B N N Y E R
T N K U R D N B A I I U S T J B C Y I I I X W E L R G R Q
E S N P Y L K I S R C R C E S M O L J O Y N G J O G Z N X
L T A U T Y L T N C D U E R A L M O S T N A S T C Y O A L
L R S L G M S B E E R E U P P S S O B N A A S N B R T T A
S U S O L Z E S A T X S G K X M N L T N P F L L D Z H I B
W C I U N G S S S N C P L R M E S E T Q M L N E W A M O O
O T G S I F T N A G I W E N E I J Y H J O V R Y R M Y N R
R O N N U K O S O C T M R R H E S L B T C E L R N O L A A
K R M L G C L H E R K S A T T K G I M L D L I L N I J L T
E N E H J T P R P C E I A T M F N M X . A E R X X D L N O
R L N R D R C N K R A H N E E N I A H N T R Z C M I M R R
Z E T U H C A R A P Y L T G L D H F I T G N I T S E T B Y
T M S P U B L I C I T Y P M S G T F A F O O L H A R D Y X
```

Jumbled Director

WENDY TAILS is the director of the not-so-classic animated movie *Hardly Working*.
But rearrange the sequence of popcorn tubs into the correct order and you'll discover the name
of a real animated movie director—slightly better known and much more successful!

Hint: The tub starts full and ends up almost empty.

___ ___ ___ ___ ___ ___ ___ ___ ___ ___

W   E   N   T   Y

D   A   I   L   S

Director Bio

I sketched my best known cartoon character while sitting on
a train. He starred in the first synchronised sound cartoon:
Steamboat Willie. I was a pioneer in animation, creating the
first colour cartoon, the first cartoon to win an Oscar as well
as the first feature length cartoon *Snow White* (it won seven
Oscars!) Although I died in 1966, my company is still one of
the biggest entertainment groups in the world.

STORYBOARD 1

Hardly is dressed ready for work.
His wife Harriet is impressed
with his style (and the fact he
dressed himself).

Picture Puzzle

Which of these ties from Hardly's closet
is he wearing?

Animation

D-Day

Hardly's had so many jobs his wife Harriet now keeps track of them using a computer database. This puzzle has a selection of the 'D' jobs. Fit the small panels back into the large grid then match the jobs with their descriptions below.

a. Designing house interiors _____

b. A motor vehicle operator _____

c. A medical practitioner _____

d. A person who sells goods _____

e. A performer who dances _____

f. A fabric and material seller _____

g. A finder of underground water _____

h. An arguer _____

i. A percussionist _____

j. A person qualified to operate on teeth _____

k. Someone who drives a herd _____

l. Person who plans healthy diets _____

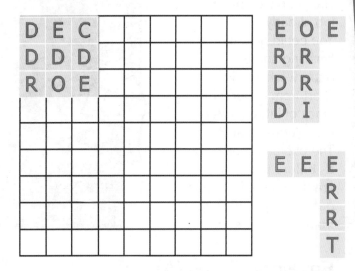

STORYBOARD 2

Hardly's in a good mood as he strides off to his first day on the job, unfortunately without his trousers.

Picture Puzzle

What's inside Hardly's BRIEF CASE?

This morning you'd find a CREAM CAKE and a FRUIT CAKE (but no LEMON CAKE). There's a DRAIN PIPE and part of a STEAM PIPE (but no WATER PIPE). Hardly also has his TRAIL BIKE and TRAIN FARE (but left his MOTOR BIKE at home).

Using the clues decide which of these items are also in his briefcase*:

1. grapevine **2.** computer **3.** whalebone **4.** green biro

*If you need help, take a really close look at the brief case.

** AEIOU = VVVVV

Animation

Desk Mess

It's only 9.30 am and Hardly's desk can hardly be seen. Has he messed this job already? You could help by finishing some paperwork for him. Start from either the stack of letters at A or the telephone at B. The choice is yours—but as before the answers are the same. So if you get stuck, just pick up from the other end!

Envelope Clues (A)

a. The event of being born. (5)

b. A person who keeps watch over something. (5)

c. To cover with too much water. (5)

d. Name of the first woman. (3)

e. Slang for toilet. (3)

f. Sea creature with pincers. (4)

g. The tissues at the base of your teeth. (4)

h. The name of Hardly's niece (see below). (5)

i. Long strip of magnetic plastic used for recording. (4)

j. A children's game where players attempt to catch the others. (3)

Telephone Clues (B)

a. Wooden door set into a wall. (4)

b. To hit lightly. (3)

c. Persistently annoy somebody. (6)

d. Large cup. (3)

e. A counter where you buy drinks. (3)

f. Neither hot nor cold. (4)

g. Not odd. (4)

h. A group of letters that makes sense. (4)

i. Unwanted cool air entering a room. (7)

j. Curved bone protecting the heart and other organs. (3)

STORYBOARD 3

`Hardly (the parachute instructor) floats gently to earth, his niece Sarah hanging on tightly to his leg.`

Picture Puzzle

Which parachute below matches Hardly's (fortunately operating!) parachute?

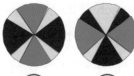

① ② ③ ④

Animation

Movie Matrix

Use the clues and the given letter to complete the movie matrix. When completed, one of the columns will answer this question:

What am I?

Spelt with no vowels, I am a precious gift given by one of the wise men to the baby Jesus at Christmas time.

subtract	**M**				
Alpine singing style		**O**			
short metal fastener			**V**		
quickly				**I**	
movable joint on doors					**E**

Pyramid Power

One of Hardly's favourite jobs was overseer on a pyramid building project. We won't mention where (or even how) the pyramid was eventually completed. Let's just say Hardly knows hardly any maths. You of course will do so much better.

To prove it, fill in the other pyramid numbers. Each stone is the sum of the two stones below it. Try starting at the light coloured stone. (What number added to 10 equals 17?)

Animation Trivia

The seven dwarfs' names in Disney's *Snow White and the Seven Dwarfs* (the first full-length animated movie) were chosen from a list of over 50, including 'Biggy', 'Hotty' and 'Shifty'.

STORYBOARD 4

With Hardly's experience with aircraft his next job finds him flying one as a crop-duster.

Picture Puzzle

Change PILOT, adding one letter at a time into:

Going up: a handgun, to be lit by a bright light and to be the most polite.

Going down: made into a mess, the top layer of earth on a garden bed, relief pilots.

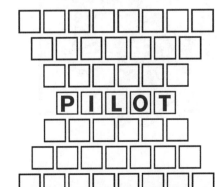

Free Advice

J R R Tolkien has some useful advice for Hardly. To decipher his words of wisdom complete each square with one of the letters in the column above. Some squares are easy to fill in (for example, when there's only one letter) but others will take skill, logic and clever guesswork. Mr Tolkien's advice may also be of use…

S	T	A		L	A	D		O	H	A		E	T	A		E	N
T	T	E	S	T	O	N	J	T	S	T	T	T	V	E	R	I	S	I	S	H

I	'	■			■		B	■	N			■			■	■	■	■
		R		E	■				■			K		■	■	■
	H	■				G	E		■		O		F				

J R R Tolkien

Hardly MD

Hardly was sacked from the hospital for a 'negative attitude'. This was a little unfair as he was working in the X-ray department at the time.

Anyhow, which of the four negatives matches Hardly?

STORYBOARD 5

Hardly takes to scuba diving like a fish to cycling.

Picture Puzzle

Hardly's job is to locate and tag endangered fish. **Angelic** fish are worth 5 points, **Freon** fish are worth 7 points and **Snuppy** fish are worth 13 points. If Hardly tagged 4 fish in total each day, how many of each fish did he tag?

	Day 1	Day 2	Day 3
Angelic			
Freon			
Snuppy			
Total Points	38	36	40

Animation

How Was Work Today?

It's a tradition in the Ployed household. Hardly arrives home, Harriet asks him how work was and… well, Hardly makes an attempt at humour. Match his side-splitting responses by writing a number next to each of Harriet's questions.

So Hardly, how was work today…

(15) I jammed my foot in a machine

(14) The boss really ticked me off.

(13) It's one crop of problems after another

(2) Terrible-I kept slipping up!

(1) Fred the boss is always needling me.

(12) Busy; my pager went non-stop.

(11) I hit a few high notes

(3) I don't think I'll see it through.

(4) I don't know; my head's still in a spin.

(5) I'm in way above my head.

(6) A real pane.

(7) Fare.

(8) I don't know weather I'll be there long.

(10) It doesn't stack up to my other jobs

(9) I've cemented some good friendships

a. … as a bricklayer? ____

b. … as a merry-go-round tester? ____

c. … as a meteorologist? ____

d. … as a swimming instructor? ____

e. … as a window washer? ____

f. … as an opera singer? ____

g. … at the chimney factory? ____

h. … at the clock shop? ____

i. … at the marmalade factory? ____

j. … at the opticians? ____

k. … down on the farm? ____

l. … in the banana shop? ____

m. … in the book shop? ____

n. … in the sewing shop? ____

o. … taxi driving? ____

STORYBOARD 6

It sounded like a dream job; lay around on your back all day doing nothing. The catch was what he was laying in ...

Picture Puzzle

Poor Hardly! For a while he was completely submerged. But by slowly moving his arms for a minute he pushes himself out 20 cm. But when he rests for the next minute he sinks back 15 cm. If Hardly is 1.8m tall, how long will it take for him to be completely out of the quicksand?

Cartoon Characters

Hidden in the grid are 12 famous cartoon characters. Each character's name is written in order, one letter to a line, starting from the top line and ending in one of the coloured squares. Use the colour-coded clues of their famous sayings (or best friends) to help.

B	T	H	S	M	S	R	B	B	R	G	F
U	N	A	W	A	R	E	I	O	U	I	O
R	O	M	A	Z	C	E	G	E	R	M	N
S	Z	O	K	E	D	B	E	D	F	T	
F	I	L	B	E	R	T	P	R	A		
Y	U	L	E	I	S	U	I	Y			
M	I	N	I	N	G	L	E				
N	O	H	M	N	N	D					
P	U	T	T	E	Y						
Y	S	S	S	R							
T	O	E	E								
A	O	N									
N	R										
E											

- Yabba Dabba Do Da!
- To infinity and beyond!
- D'oh
- Minnie Mouse
- Beep Beep!
- What's up doc?
- Odie
- I tawt I taw a puddy tat!
- Charlie Brown
- Roar!
- Don't have a cow!
- Stimpy

STORYBOARD 7

This is Hardly's favourite job; stunt man on the set of 'Super Santa's Skateboard Surprise'.

Picture Puzzle

Each of these five paths has the letters SANTA. But one path has an extra letter. Which one?

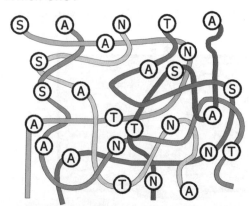

Animation

What's My Job?

Rearrange the letters in the grid to spell out this job title.

T	A	M
A	N	I
O	R	S

We create animated films. Some of us make and photograph clay models, others paint plastic celluloids and film them in sequence but most of us use a computer to generate 3D characters and settings. To make animated characters more realistic we can use motion-capture equipment to record human movement on the computer.

___ ___ ___ ___ ___ ___ ___ ___ ___

ROW + DS = WORDS

Each answer to the clues below is an anagram of the word ROW plus one of the ten pairs of letters. Hardly has done the first one for you (which is hardly a good start).

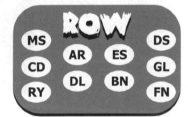

ROW

MS CD RY AR DL ES BN DS GL FN

1. Pointed flying weapon <u>ARROW</u>

2. Colour _____

3. Large group of people _____

4. Concern _____

5. Squishy, soft-bodied living creatures _____

6. Sharp edged weapon _____

7. Low rumbling sound _____

8. Facial expression of dislike _____

9. The Earth _____

10. Said rude words _____

STORYBOARD 8

`Head-tester in a toy bows-and-arrows factory goes exactly as Hardly imagines it will.`

Picture Puzzle

How many arrows actually hit Hardly? Follow the three paths from the Start. Cross out each arrow between the 'S' and the three coloured circles. Count the number of arrows remaining.

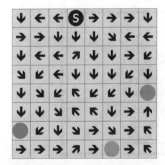

Hollywood Crossquiz

Oo oo! Nine 'oo' words needed to complete the Hollywood experience. Use the clues, fill in the blanks.

Clue								
Thug, young criminal	**H**	O	O					
Someone who looks on	**O**			O	O			
Metal ring that forms a hole	**L**	O	O					
Make less tight	**L**	O	O					
Popular American civil war song	**Y**						O	O
Fluffy	**W**	O	O					
Leaking through a small opening	**O**	O						
To aim too high above a target	**O**					O	O	
To let saliva drip from the mouth (yuck!)	**D**		O	O				

Brick Out

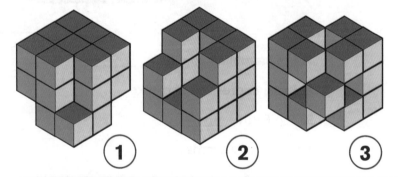

Hardly's bricklaying leaves a lot to be desired! Here are three cubes he's built. Each is supposed to have 27 (3x3x3) bricks. How many does each actually have?
Hint: No 'hidden' bricks are missing.

STORYBOARD 9

Construction work suits Hardly down to the ground. Or rather, into the ground...

Picture Puzzle

Which of these four nets can't be folded into a pretend brick?

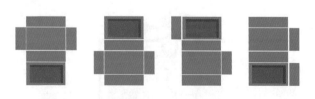

Animation

Hardly Heaven

Hardly's last job (at least for this film) is playing guitar up by the Pearly Gates. Write each letter in its connecting circle to discover the song he's playing.

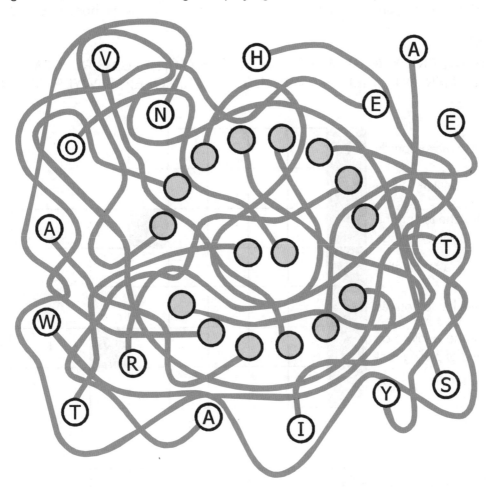

STORYBOARD 10

`Oh dear... looks like Hardly's`
`last job was really his last`
`job. On Earth, anyway.`

Picture Puzzle

Hardly has learnt four chords to play on his guitar. Look at the four chord diagrams (beloved of guitarists everywhere). Now if you know that the vertical lines are strings, the horizontal lines are frets (the metal bars across a guitar's neck) and that the black circles are where you put your fingers, can you work out which of the diagrams is wrong?

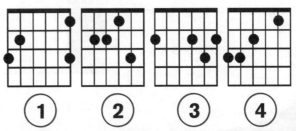

Unusual Occupations

Many jobs that were common a hundred years ago are now completely unknown. Match up the list of jobs to the job descriptions (and the number of blank squares). When complete, the brown column will spell out the (unusual!) job title of an artist who carves ivory, bone or wood.

Word List

CAPER, CHOWDER, EYER, GLIMMER MAN, HANKYMAN, HELLO GIRL, ICEMAN, MONDAY MAN, NIMGIMMER, OUTCRIER, PLUMBUM, RATONER, ROPER, SAWYER, SPOONER

saws up timber to make boards

makes capes

operates the telephone exchange

a rat catcher

delivers ice to houses

works for the landlord on Mondays instead of paying rent

a plumber

makes spoons

sells fish

a travelling magician

an auctioneer

a doctor

turns down the gas lights in Dublin

makes the eyes in needles

makes ropes and nets

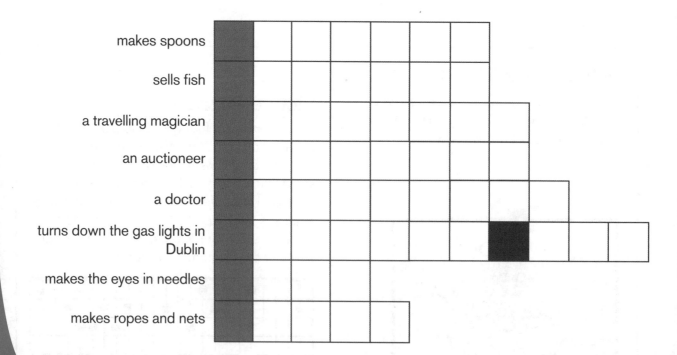

Animation

Flip Book

Yes, it's true; you too can have your very own, limited edition Hardly Working flip book! Simply cut out the cartoon sequence below, assemble (in order) into a booklet then carefully staple along the left-hand side. Hold the book's spine in your left hand then let the pages flip over using your right hand. (If you're left-handed, try stapling the book on the right and reversing the hand positions.)

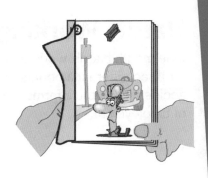

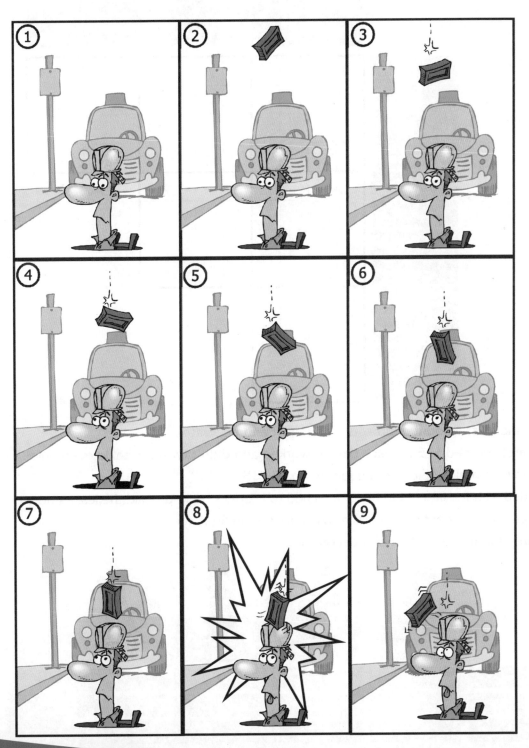

Hardly Working

One month Hardly worked in four different jobs and received four different salaries. He worked for three different amounts of time (he had two jobs in one day) and each job ended in a different accident. Use the information given to match the jobs, the salaries, the accidents and the length of employment.

	one day	one day	weekend	one week	false teeth	paper cut	twisted ankle	wallpaper glue	$0.15	$1.50	$15.00	$150.00
dancer												
decorator												
dentist												
dramatist												
$0.15												
$1.50												
$15.00												
$150.00												
false teeth												
paper cut												
twisted ankle												
wallpaper glue												

1. Hardly worked the least amount of time as a dramatist and decorator.

2. As a dancer, Hardly earned $75 for each day he worked and didn't twist his ankle even once.

3. Wallpaper glue was a real problem in the job that paid $15.

4. The job that ended with the false teeth firmly attached to Hardly's backside paid the least amount.

5. Hardly's average pay as a dentist was 20c a day (and 30c on Sunday).

6. He earned more as a dramatist than as a decorator

	Dancer	Decorator	Dentist	Dramatist
Salary				
Accident				
Length of Employment				

Animation

The Hardly Working® Trivia Quiz

Welcome, welcome and welcome to the 'Hardly Working' trivia quiz. It's probably not a bad idea to have actually completed the puzzles in this chapter first but, if not, well your undoubtedly low scoring result will be our little secret. Mostly.

Instructions

Don't use a calculator. Don't use a dictionary.
Don't cheat by turning back to find the answers.
Don't cheat by turning forward to look at the answers.

1. What is Hardly's wife's name?
   (a) Harold
   (b) Harry
   (c) Harriet
   (d) Harpo

2. Name Mickey Mouse's first cartoon with sound.
   (a) Tugboat Timmy
   (b) Cruise Ship Carson
   (c) Steamboat Willie
   (d) Pirate Ship Pete

3. What did Hardly forget on his first day of work?
   (a) His lunch
   (b) His mobile phone
   (c) His pants
   (d) His glasses

4. Which of these items wasn't on Hardly's desk?
   (a) A lease
   (b) A telephone
   (c) A sandwich
   (d) A pile of envelopes

5. What did Hardly get to oversee the building of?
   (a) The Leaning Tower of Pisa
   (b) The Sydney Harbour Bridge
   (c) The Great Pyramid
   (d) The Great Wall of China

6. What did Hardly have to do to the fish he caught?
   (a) Paint them
   (b) Eat them
   (c) Tag them
   (d) Play Go Fish

7. What was written on the 'Danger' sign at the quicksand testing ground?
   (a) Quicksand
   (b) Stand Here
   (c) Danger
   (d) No Smoking

8. What is written on the stunt Santa's shorts?
   (a) Merry Christmas
   (b) Eat My Shorts
   (c) Ho Ho Ho
   (d) Rudolph

9. Where was Hardly when the brick fell on his head?
   (a) In a brick-making factory
   (b) On a brick-firing range
   (c) Down a hole in the road
   (d) Brixton

10. What instrument was Hardly given to play in heaven?
    (a) A harp
    (b) An accordion
    (c) A guitar
    (d) A xylophone

Learning More

TOONS

Don Markstein's Toonopedia
www.toonopedia.com

Disney
disney.go.com

Pixar
www.pixar.com

Looney Tunes
looneytunes.com

HOME ANIMATION

Cartoonster: make-your-own cartoon tutorials
www.kidzdom.com/tutorials

Cartoon Smart
www.cartoonsmart.com

Post-It Note animations
www.bigempire.com/postittheater

Flip Books
www.abc.net.au/creaturefeatures/make/flipbook.htm

JOBS

What Interests You?
www.bls.gov/k12

Women's Professions
www.womenswork.org/girls/careers.html

Soundtrack

Everything you hear in a movie is part of the **soundtrack**. The soundtrack has three separate groups of sounds:

Voice

1. **Narration** is script said by a character off-screen or what an onscreen character is thinking.

2. **Dialogue** is script said by the onscreen characters, usually to each other.

Sound Effects (FX)

3. **Synchronous** sound effects happen in time with onscreen action.

4. **Asynchronous** sound effects are background sounds such as office noises, wind or traffic sounds.

Music

5. **Background** music is music played for dramatic effect.

6. **Local** music is music heard by (or made by) the onscreen characters.

Script to Soundtrack

Match these parts of the script to the different soundtrack parts:

1. *FX of typewriters, adding machines and chatter.*　　　　　1. _____

2. VOICE-OVER　　**It was another boring day in the office…**　2. _____

3. DIANNE　　*(Taps pencil on desk and sighs)*　　　　　　　3. _____

4.　　**What a boring day at the office.**　　　　　　　　　　4. _____

5. *A brass band enters playing a rousing march.*　　　　　　5. _____

6. ROGER　　**What a rousing march! I must whistle!**　　　　6. _____

7. *FX of brass band falling down the stairs.*　　　　　　　　7. _____

8. DIANNE　　*(Yawns)*　　　　　　　　　　　　　　　　　8. _____

9.　　**Nothing ever happens around here!**　　　　　　　　　9. _____

10. *FX of dramatic organ chord as the lights go out…*　　　　10. _____

FILM SCHEME
sound & music

Instrument Squares

There are 11 instruments in these squares. What's in the mystery square? Identify each instrument and find its line in the solution below. Write the given letter of the instrument's name in the square. For example, write the instrument in D3 on the first line, writing its first letter in the square.
When completed, the squares will spell out an instrument that can sound like all the other instruments.

Instruments:

bassoon, cymbal, drums, flute, guitar, piano, saxophone, trombone, trumpet, violin, washboard

D3	☐	1 _____
B1	____ ☐	2 _____
B2 _____	☐	6
B3	☐	1 _____
D2	____ ☐	4
A1 _____	☐	5
C1	____ ☐	4 _____
C3	____ ☐	2 _____
C2 _____	☐	5
A3 _____	☐	8
A2 _____	☐	6

① ② ③

A
B
C
D ?

PROJECT

Soundtrack Study

Watch five minutes of an interesting movie. Which of these do you hear? Write a tick for each one you recognise.

Movie Title _____

1. Narration ☐☐☐☐	4. Asynchronous sound effects ☐☐☐☐
2. Dialogue ☐☐☐☐	5. Background music ☐☐☐☐
3. Synchronous sound effects ☐☐☐☐	6. Local music ☐☐☐☐

Musicians

1. Who was the film's music **composer** (creates the music)? _____

2. Who was the music **arranger** (writes the music out for playing)? _____

3. Were any songs used as background music? Name one. _____

41

Back to Front (the musical)

GMG decide a comedy-musical will be a huge box office success and film *Back to Front,* a movie based on the comeback tour of the famous '70s rock group, the Backroom Band.

Band Names

In the movie the Backroom Band members spend considerable time deciding on a band name. Before finally deciding on one they write out this list of possibilities. It didn't help; they like all of them except for one. Which one do you think it was? Why?

MACRO BOK	MABO ROCK	ROCK AMBO
BAM CROOK	MOCK BOAR	COB KORMA
RAK COMBO	BOOK MARC	MAB CROAK
MOK COBRA	MOCK BORA	BROO MACK

Genre Buster

Movie musicals (such as *Grease*) are usually based on stage musicals. These movies often have spectacular dance scenes and the songs' lyrics help tell the story.

Music movies (such as *School of Rock*) also have lots of music. In these movies though, the songs aren't as important and the lyrics don't help tell the story.

The early years of rock 'n' roll saw many new music movies filmed. Elvis Presley alone starred in over 30 such movies, including *Jailhouse Rock* and *Viva Las Vegas*.

Movie Music Trivia

The first talking/singing movie was *The Jazz Singer* in 1927 and starred Al Jolson. The first stage musical to be made into a film was *Showboat* in 1929. The first full-length animated movie musical was Walt Disney's *Snow White and the Seven Dwarfs*.

Magic-band Magic-square

Five of the words from this paragraph can be used to fill the grid below so that it reads the same vertically and horizontally.

In the film the Backroom Band tours Australia and visits Uluru where they have a super time viewing the changing colours. After a brief stop in Alice Springs to pick up Irene, the lead singer's mum (recently cured of an ingrown toenail), they head north for a music concert in Darwin.

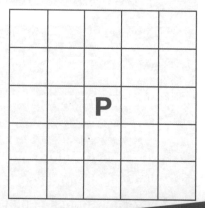

Music

Poster Posers

The answers to these puzzles are on the poster.

Anagrammaticals

The Backroom Band's members are featured on the poster singing or playing an instrument. But each of them also has another role in the band. To find out their second musical talent look more closely at their names:

1. Who also plays LEAD GUITAR?

_____

2. Who also performs LEAD VOCALS?

_____

3. Who also plays BASS GUITAR?

_____

4. Who also plays PERCUSSION?

_____

5. Who also plays KEYBOARDS?

_____

Capital Sentence

Back to Front (the musical) was filmed on location around the world. Which of these cities is one of the 'many more'?: **Ottawa**, **Tokyo**, **Moscow** or **Manila**?

Hint: Look for a pattern among the capital cities mentioned on the poster.

Synopsis Search

This puzzle will help you answer the age-old question:
what is a drummer?

Instructions

1. Read the short synopsis then find and cross out each word in the grid. Only look for words of four letters or more. Hyphens and apostrophes have been removed.

2. When you finish, write in order from left to right the first 31 leftover letters in the spaces below.

___ ___ ___ ___ ___ ___ ___ ___ ___ ___ ___ ___

___ ___ ___ ___ ___ ___ ___ ___ ___ ___ ___ ___ ___ ___ .

In the wild seventies they had it all: fame, fortune and an international tour. But the lead act, 'The Bananas', split in Barbados, leaving the Backroomers out of money, out of luck and straight out of pop's revolving door. Thirty years later they're back, as headliners for a huge rock nostalgia concert. But can these aging stars recapture their earlier brilliance? Can Pu and Gu stop arguing over Dosy's affections? Can Guab finally get her hair cut? And, most importantly, will Dallas get the lyrics right to the chorus of the number one hit, *Back-dated*? Find out, in GMG's great new comedy-musical!

```
A P E B A U G R Y T R I H T R S O N W B T H R O H A
N S E V E N T I E S G B S O L E P N A L S H U I T W
N O S T A L G I A I T H A A M O I C U G A T G U A S
I C K C U L I A N S T R N C P S K L R M Q T A I F H
S A N A N A B R R R B O M S K R C E R Y B G E R R E
H C O M E D Y M U S I C A L O M A I S A J E S R S C
L Y T T S Y S O D T Y W R O E T B C R E E N R G R N
Q E L N Y T E S A L L E M S M S A F L Y H K A M E A
D N E M F R U N L E C E T T A N C S O L L T E G N I
A O O A G Y R R A A A R R I E F O K Z O R I T Y S I L
L M D E O E N V P S A L G B S I D C Y D T W R K L L
L D H H T I I T X I P U D Q T T A V O B A U T T D I
A T C N F N U G G S H O N D O C T F I N D B N Q A R
S M I R G R N H P M O L B D P E E M R O C W R E E B
N K T X E I T Y L R I E H T R F D Y W V D E I A H Y
M C O N G H A R G U I N G D B F Q Z C E R H R L B E
X O U A G N I V O L O V E R T L A N N Y R T H Z T D H
F R R J M O S T G F I M P O R T A N T L Y M R N N T
```

Music

Turn It Up

The Backroom Band's power amplifier has some quite unusual settings. Look at each row of dials and decide what the next setting would be. Write it in the white circle.

Hints:

(A) Some concerts seem to go on for **WEEKS**…

(B) The movie is shown on **PRIME** time TV

(C) And some concerts go on for **MONTHS**!

(D) That gap is getting too much bigger all the time…

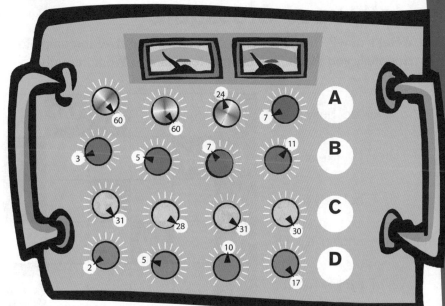

Movie Matrix

Use the clues and the given letters to complete the movie matrix. When completed, one of the columns will answer this question:

What am I?

I am a type of starling with a colourful beak. I can mimic animal sounds and human speech but am considered a pest in some parts of the world.

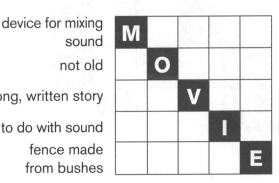

clue				
device for mixing sound	M			
not old		O		
long, written story			V	
having to do with sound				I
fence made from bushes					E

STORYBOARD 1

The Backroom Band drive their trusty Band-mobile through the stormy night to prepare for the concert in Timberstash.

Picture Puzzle

Look at the peace sign on the side of the band-mobile. See if you can draw it in one continuous line, without retracing or taking your pen off the paper.

Hollywood Crossquiz

WHat's new? The nine words containing H and W to complete our Hollywood quiz, that's **WH**at! **H**opefully you **W**on't find this one too **H**ard to **W**ork through.

Clue	Grid
wide, busy road	**H** · · **H W** ·
like an owl	**O W** · · · **H**
not very heavy	**L** · · **H** · **W** · · **H** ·
not high sounding in pitch	**L** · **W** · · · **H** ·
of a yellow colour	**Y** · · · · **W** · · **H**
white paint from lime and water	**W H** · · · **W** · · **H**
remove someone from power by force	**O** · · · · **H** · · **W**
too heavy for being in good health	**O** · · · **W** · · · **H**
machine for washing dishes	**D** · · **H W** · · **H** ·

STORYBOARD 2

The band discovers the concert site is flooded. They decide the show must go on regardless.

Picture Puzzle

What a shame nobody in the band could read a weather chart…

See if you could have done any better using your knowledge (and logic) to match these weather symbols with their meanings.

(a) fog (b) light rain (c) lightning
(d) moderate snow (e) smoke/smog
(f) thunderstorm (g) thunderstorm with rain
(h) tornado

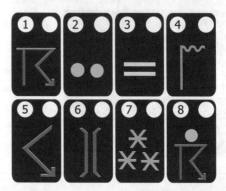

Music

Jumbled Director

Back To Front was directed by GMG's top musical director Ken Serradilla. Rearrange this sequence of movie stills into the correct order and you'll find the name of a much more successful director.

Hint: The wall starts off empty (R)… band posters appear… band members walk by… finally the wardrobe passes (R).

___ ___ ___ ___ ___ ___ ___   ___ ___ ___ ___ ___ ___ ___ ___ ___

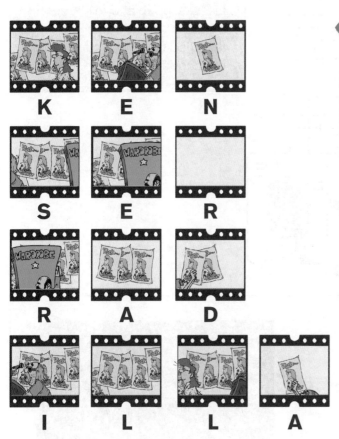

K E N

S E R

R A D

I L L A

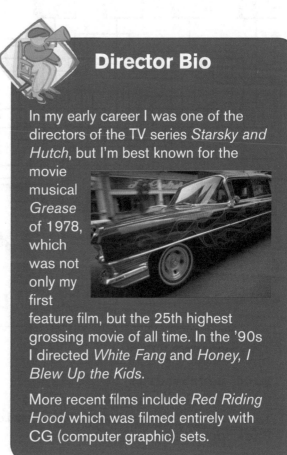

Director Bio

In my early career I was one of the directors of the TV series *Starsky and Hutch*, but I'm best known for the movie musical *Grease* of 1978, which was not only my first feature film, but the 25th highest grossing movie of all time. In the '90s I directed *White Fang* and *Honey, I Blew Up the Kids*.

More recent films include *Red Riding Hood* which was filmed entirely with CG (computer graphic) sets.

STORYBOARD 3

The crowd for the concert begins to grow—and so do the queues for the portable toilets.

Picture Puzzle

Here's an easy one; which toilet is empty?

Damp-Amp

Match these five rock musicians to their amplifiers. Which one is about to get fried?

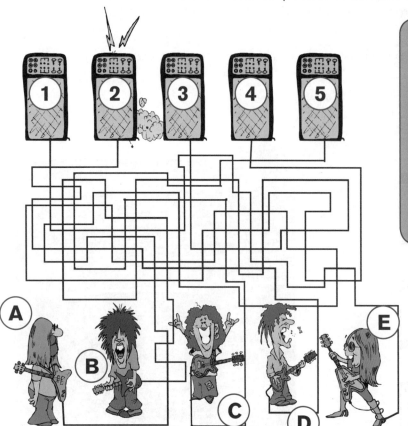

Movie Music Trivia

The Sound of Music is the most profitable box office movie musical of all time.
While filming one dance number the actress playing Liesel slipped and fell through a pane of glass. The scene then had to be re-shot with her bandaged leg covered.

STORYBOARD 4

Band merchandise is selling well to the fans who snap up t-shirts, banners and authentic Backroom Band hot-dogs.

Picture Puzzle

Uh-oh! Fake band t-shirts have been discovered! As well as the obvious spelling mistake all the shirts have the same barcode. So which one of these five barcodes is off a rip-off shirt?

MADE IN OZTRAYLEEA

(1)

(2)

(3)

(4)

(5)

Music

What's My Job?

Rearrange the letters in the grid to spell out this job title. Use each of the purple square letters three times.

S	N	G
O	E	U
D	I	R

I set up and operate sound recording equipment on the set. I'm involved in recording sound effects, dialogue and music.

__ __ __ __ __ __   __ __ __ __ __ __

Cold as Christmas

The Backroom Band's Christmas CD was a huge seller, despite the fact that nobody could work out what the songs were. Why? Because the band decided to change all the song titles. Here are five of the better known Christmas songs they recorded. What are their real names?

1. 'Metallic tinkle of objects with a ringing sound.'   __ __ __ __ __ __   __ __ __ __ __ __

2. 'A figure of a person made of packed white crystals of frozen water who goes by the name of a temperature that is pleasantly cold and invigorating.'

   __ __ __ __ __ __ __   __ __ __   __ __ __ __ __ __ __ __

3. 'The twelve rotations of the earth on its axis that make up the Christian festival celebrating the birth of Christ.'

   __ __ __   __ __ __ __ __ __   __ __ __ __   __ __   __ __ __ __ __ __ __ __ __

4. 'Utterly quiet daily period of darkness.'   __ __ __ __ __ __   __ __ __ __ __

5. 'The plural of "I" express a hope for the period of time between December 24th and January 6th to be full of high-spirited fun.'

   __ __   __ __ __ __   __ __ __   __ __ __ __ __   __ __ __ __ __ __ __

STORYBOARD 5

The roadies prepare the stage, setting up the lighting and sound systems.

```
O E E   E
T E R E I N G
T H S T I N G
T N S T T W O
```

Picture Puzzle

What is the sound guy saying to the lighting guy?

Drop the letters down into the grid (in the correct places of course) to find out.

Fussy Eaters

The Backroom Band demand only the best when touring. Part of their extensive contract stipulates the foods that each band member must have available to them backstage before (and after) each show. Three foods from each musician's dietary demands are listed. Decide where these five foods should go:

1. waffles
2. chowder
3. red mandarins
4. rabbit
5. swordfish

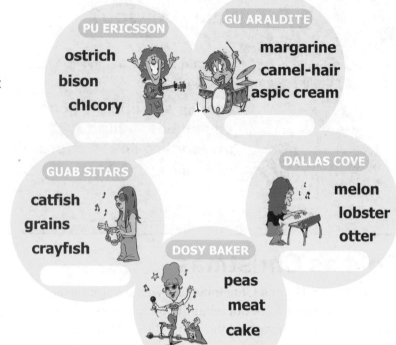

PU ERICSSON
ostrich
bison
chicory

GU ARALDITE
margarine
camel-hair
aspic cream

GUAB SITARS
catfish
grains
crayfish

DALLAS COVE
melon
lobster
otter

DOSY BAKER
peas
meat
cake

STORYBOARD 6

The sound mixer is having problems with screeching, painful feedback from the microphones. Or is it just the lead singer's voice?

Picture Puzzle

The technician needs to mute all the number 5 buttons. But which ones are they? Use the following information to locate them. Then write the four buttons in the squares below.

1. Each row has five buttons numbered 1-5. No row is in the correct order. The number one buttons are already written in for you.

2. Each column has four buttons. No column has two buttons with the same number. The total of each column is shown below the grid.

3. The sum of buttons A2 and A3 equal button A5. The sum of buttons B2 and B5 equal button B4.

	1	2	3	4	5
A	1				
B			1		
C				1	
D					1
	10	14	11	12	13

Music

Ralph the Roadie

Wind Me Up

Four of these guitar leads were wound up by Ralph the Roadie.
Which one wasn't?

Last Lead

And talking of Ralph: which of these seven guitar leads did he
put down last?

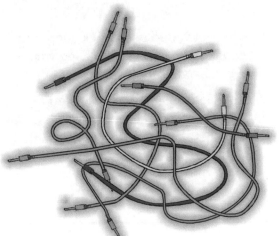

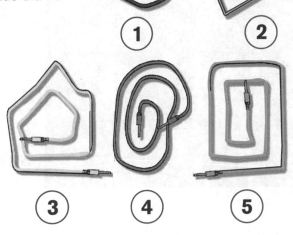

STORYBOARD 7

The crowd sings along with all
the words to the song.

Picture Puzzle

The words to the song really aren't that complicated, consisting mainly of the words 'you',
'do' and 'love'. Reassemble the lyrics in the grid provided using the marked black squares
to help.

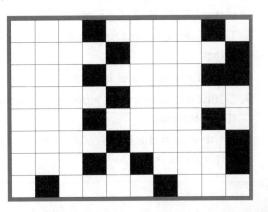

Take Your Pick

Ralph keeps the band members' guitar picks (also known as plectrums) in a special custom-made wooden box. But which two of the five numbered guitar picks are missing from the box?

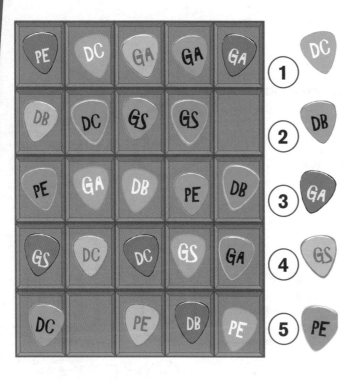

1 DC

2 DB

3 GA

4 GS

5 PE

Movie Music Trivia

The first film to use a rock song was *Blackboard Jungle*. The song was *Rock Around the Clock*.

The Beatles made an animated movie musical called *Yellow Submarine* in 1968.

STORYBOARD 8

Despite the muddy conditions the crowd dances (and meditates) to the happening sounds of the MAHARAJAS, GIBBLE-GABBLE, CLICK-CLACK, SKEDADDLED and SQUEEGEE.

Picture Puzzle

The cool dude meditating is thinking deep thoughts about his favourite band. Catch his brainwaves and guess what it is…

1. Think of a number between 2 and 10.

2. Multiply it by 9.

3. Add the two digits together.

4. Add 1 and convert the number to a letter (A=1, B=2, C=3 etc).

5. Think of a country beginning with your letter.

6. Find the last vowel in its name.

7. Count forward in the alphabet a further three letters.

8. Write down the band with four of that letter in its name.

Music

Band Names

Hidden in this grid are 16 four-letter band names. Eight are written, in correct letter sequence, horizontally and eight are written, also in correct letter sequence, vertically. To find them, 'slide' a strip from the left onto the grid. When the blank spaces correspond with a word, lightly shade in the grey squares on the grid and write the word below. When you finish, the shaded squares will reveal the vertical words.

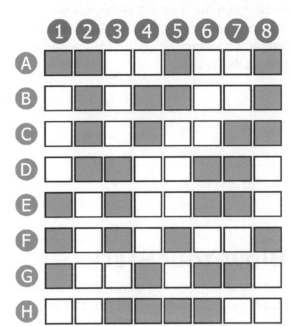

STORYBOARD 9

Pu's first (and unfortunately last) attempt at crowd surfing goes disastrously wrong.

Picture Puzzle

The people in the crowd appear to be calling out rather strange words for a concert. But what they're really shouting out is four names, each of five letters. Person 1 has shouted out the first letters of the names (JABS). Person 2 has shouted out the jumbled-up *second* letters of the names (RAIL), person 3 has shouted out the jumbled-up *third* letters of the names and so on. Write the four names below.

Hint: There are two boys' and two girls' names.

J _ _ _ _

A _ _ _ _

B _ _ _ _

S _ _ _ _

Rock Around the Clock

This clock (with only 9 numbers) has the letter K in its centre. That's because if you arrange the groups of letters correctly into their four squares they'll make a five-letter word that ends in K. But that's not all. If you write down the 9 letters in the yellow squares, you'll reveal the name of the band leader who sang the song with the same title as this puzzle.

— — — — — — — — —

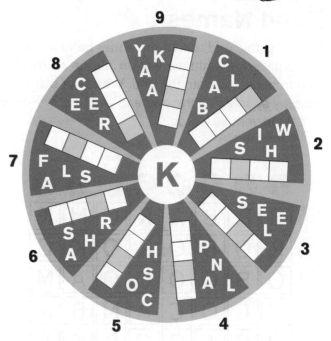

Blow Your Stack

The speaker stack has blown three speakers and Ralph the Roadie has to find and fix 'em. Use his clues to find the three malfunctioning units.

1. None of the blown speakers are in the same row or column.

2. Column 5 is okay.

3. There are four healthy speakers next to each other in row C.

4. Column 4 is okay.

5. The broken row B speaker is in an even column.

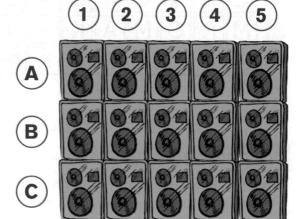

STORYBOARD 10

`And after the show... the huge cleanup.`

Picture Puzzle

Bruno the cleaner is paid by the hour for cleaning the concert area. To make the job last longer, he occasionally empties his bag and starts again. Which is the only piece of rubbish he hasn't already collected before?

Music

Hit and Miss

When bands used to release records instead of CDs they had to decide which side of the single was the 'A side' (the hit) and which was the 'B side' (not the hit). You have a similar decision to make. Will you try the A side clues or the B side clues? The choice is yours—but the answers are the same. So work out the clues and write the answers on the circles with the A answers starting from the left. And if you get stuck—write the B answers starting from the right. Oh, and since all the clues are from Backroom Band lyrics, there are rhyming words to help you out.

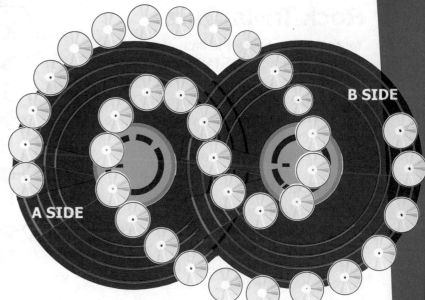

A SIDE

B SIDE

A Side Clues

(a) Look at my frown it won't disappear, Look at me here I'll ___ ___ ___ ___ ___ in my tears. (5)

(b) I can't believe it now, we had a ___ ___ ___. (3)

(c) You're the only one for me, can't you ___ ___ ___ ? (3)

(d) I'm not a rat, I'm not a cat, I'm not a gnat, I'm just a ___ ___ ___ . (3)

(e) Don't get me down, don't ___ ___ ___ me frown. (3)

(f) Rest In Peace is RIP, Over Head Projector is ___ ___ ___ (abbrv). (3)

(g) I ___ ___ ___ my baby walkin', a walkin' on her own. (3)

(h) I hoped he wasn't hurt when he fell in the ___ ___ ___ ___. (4)

(i) Let's take a picnic down to the park, with a lettuce ___ ___ ___ ___ ___, we'll eat 'til dark. (5)

(j) So you're tired, take a ___ ___ ___, while you're sleepin', I'll read the map. (3)

B Side Clues

(a) Eating bamboo, he doesn't care, he's a great big ___ ___ ___ ___ ___ bear. (5)

(b) You ain't the first, you ain't the ___ ___ ___ ___, I'm leavin' you behind so fast. (4)

(c) I'm ___ ___ ___ of you, oh yes you're gone, Oh yes, you're finished, just like this song. (3)

(d) I'm in love, love stung me good, stung me like a ___ ___ ___ ___, it's stung me good. (4)

(e) I've got one house on Park Lane left to sell, and after that I've just got one ___ ___ ___ ___ ___. (5)

(f) I'd like to thank my lovin' ma and pa, So thank you mum, and to my dad, well ___ ___. (2)

(g) I was stung before by love way back in D, I'm stung again, but this time by some ___ ___ ___ ___. (4)

(h) My jeans have patches, they're so ___ ___ ___ ___ and torn, just like me they feel so all forlorn. (4)

(i) What are you saying, what have you heard? What is the verdict, what is the ___ ___ ___ ___? (4)

Music

Rock Trivia Quiz

Your task is to follow the path of red and blue arrows from the START to one of the four CDs. You'll then head out via its black arrow and end at a second CD. If you follow the correct trail you'll know the name of the Backroom Band's support act (and the city they're from).

Instructions

Read the START question below. If you think the RED answer is correct, follow the RED arrow from the start hexagon to the letter S. If you think the BLUE answer is correct, follow the BLUE arrow to the letter L. Look up the question belonging to the letter you're on and choose RED or BLUE again. Keep in mind there is only one correct path, so if the answer doesn't make sense then check those questions again!

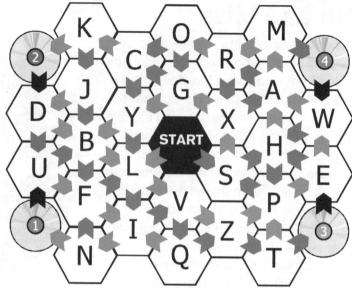

Band Name: _ _ _ _ _ _ _ _ _ _ **City:** _ _ _ _ _ _ _ _ _ **CDs:** __ and __

		guitar	saxophone
	The most important rock instrument is the		
A	The first big rock 'n' roll hit was	Waltzing Matilda	Rock Around the Clock
B	Bob Dylan sang	heavy metal	folk rock
C	Motown Records (in Detroit) was short for	Monster Tone	Motor Town
D	The Beatles toured the USA in	1964	1935
E	Woodstock was a famous	rock concert	racing horse
F	Music Videos were introduced in 1981 by	ABC	MTV
G	The biggest selling rock album was	Empty Chairs	Thriller
H	DJ is an abbreviation of	Don't Jump	Disc Jockey
I	The Rolling Stones came from	The Himalayas	The UK
J	PA is an abbreviation of	Public Address	Perfect Acoustics
K	The Beach Boys' surf sound came from	The Gold Coast	California
L	Jimi Hendrix was famous for his	guitar solos	trumpet solos
M	Rock 'n' roller Chuck Berry played	keyboards	lead guitar
N	The most popular dance style of the 1970s was	the tango	disco
O	A standard rock band has drums, lead, rhythm and	bass guitar	acoustic guitar
P	AC/DC is a hard rock band from	Australia	Scotland
Q	Rap music began in the mid	1970s	1990s
R	Elvis Presley's first record was released by	Moon Records	Sun Records
S	Rock 'n' Roll started in the	1950s	1970s
T	Techno music is generated using	dice	computers
U	Reggae music started in	Jamaica	Japan
V	IPods are music players made by	IBM	Apple
W	Smoke on the Water is by	Deep Purple	The Beatles
X	A bass guitar has	Seven strings	Four strings
Y	Fender, Les Paul and Gibson are all brands of	guitar	American cars
Z	LP is an abbreviation for	long playing	loud party

56

Music

Music to Go

Dallas listens to a lot of music on his mp3 player, a very fashionable 'Ppod' player. One evening after band practice he notices that the first five **song titles** on his playlist all have a musical instrument hidden in their titles.

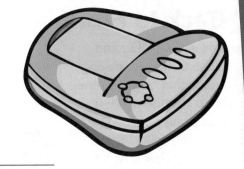

1. Find each one and write it in on the line.

THE BANGUI TARENTELLA by TV MAN AWAY _____

RAZOR SHARP by VAGUE LOIS _____

CYBORG ANTHEM by ANT'S DIARY _____

SWINE FLU TEQUILA by IDLE DRIFT _____

RED RUM RUMBLE by FANCY THAT! _____

2. Write the five instruments in alphabetical order in the rectangles below.

3. Write each instrument's matching band name in the nine squares.

4. Reading down and up you should now be able to see Dallas's favourite song spelt out for you. Write it on the dashes.

_ _ _ _ _ _ _ _ _ _ _ _ _ _ _ _ _ _

Like Peas in a Pod

Dallas loves his Ppod player. In fact he likes it so much he's bought five identical units. Well, almost identical. What is the one feature on each player different from the rest?

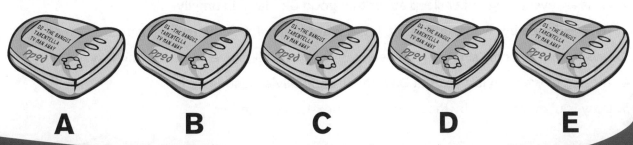

A   **B**   **C**   **D**   **E**

Back to Front

Dallas, Dosy, Gu and Guab all have annoying habits that bug the other band members when they're on tour.
Each musician used to be in a band with a 'pongy' name and each can sing up to a certain note (before they sound like cackling hyenas). Use the clues to match the information to each band member.

Movie Musical Trivia

Musical movies of the 1970s included *Jesus Christ Superstar* (1973), *The Rocky Horror Picture Show* (1975), *Saturday Night Fever* (1977) and *Grease* (1978).

	eats garlic	snores loudly	talks in sleep	always tapping	Stinky	Icky	Smelly	Funky	C	D	E	G
Dallas												
Dosy												
Gu												
Guab												
C												
D												
E												
G												
Stinky												
Icky												
Smelly												
Funky												

C D E G

musical notes

	Dallas	Dosy	Gu	Guab
Annoying habit on tour				
Highest note they can sing				
Previous band				

1. Gu is always talking in her sleep about the 'good old days' in Smelly.

2. The band member who can sing the highest absolutely loves the taste of garlic.

3. Dallas (who can only sing a C) has been tapping his fingers ever since leaving Icky.

4. The singer who can just reach a D wrote all of Smelly's hit songs.

5. Dosy is often annoyed by the snoring of the ex-Funky member.

Music

The Back to Front®
Trivia Quiz

Welcome to the last page in this chapter. Like the chapters that have preceded it, and the ones to follow, we present a trivia quiz based on the film this chapter is based on. Actually doing the puzzles before doing this quiz is a good idea but, hey, if you don't want to follow our advice, be it on your own head.

Instructions

Sigh. You need instructions? For a quiz? Is this book maybe a little too hard? Well, if we must then… Read the questions. Circle the answers. Don't cheat.

1. What colour is the guitar on the 'Back to Front' logo?
   (a) Greenish
   (b) Blueish
   (c) Reddish
   (d) Purplish

2. Which of these places wasn't a location the film was shot in?
   (a) Athens
   (b) Madrid
   (c) New York
   (d) Stockholm

3. What was painted on the side of the Band-mobile?
   (a) A musical note
   (b) Keep Out
   (c) A peace sign
   (d) The band's name

4. What famous film musical did Randal Kleiser direct?
   (a) Chicago
   (b) The Sound of Music
   (c) Grease
   (d) My Fair Lady

5. What food was available next to the T-Shirt stand at the concert?
   (a) Tacos
   (b) Hamburgers
   (c) Hot dogs
   (d) Fried chicken

6. What is on the cover of the band's Christmas CD?
   (a) Santa
   (b) Reindeer
   (c) A star
   (d) Presents

7. Where was the sound mixer standing to mix the concert?
   (a) On the stage
   (b) Behind the stage
   (c) In front of the stage
   (d) By the side of the stage

8. Which way does Ralph the Roadie wind the guitar leads?
   (a) Messily
   (b) Clockwise
   (c) Anti-clockwise
   (d) Pointing north

9. What is a plectrum?
   (a) A stand for the drum kit
   (b) A musical note
   (c) A guitar pick
   (d) A distorted sound

10. How many speakers were blown in the stack?
   (a) None
   (b) All of them
   (c) Three
   (d) Seven, but it recovered

Learning More

MUSICALS

www.musicals.net

History of Film Musicals
www.musicals101.com/erafilm.htm

Grease – UK musical site
www.greasethemusical.co.uk

ROCK MUSIC

All Music Guide
www.allmusic.com

Australian Rock Music
www.abc.net.au/longway

The Rock Hall of Fame
www.rockhall.com

MAKING MUSIC

DJ Turntables online
www.turntables.de

Write your own rap
www.bbc.co.uk/education/listenandwrite/raprealm

Recording Studio
www.bbc.co.uk/musiclive/commonwealth

Blast Music Machine
www.bbc.co.uk/blast/music

FILM SCHOOL

stunts

Stunt Puzzler 1

How many stunt planes does each own?

Stella _____   Stan _____

Stunt Puzzler 2

Put the stunt actors in order of their years of experience (from most to least).

1. _____ 2. _____ 3. _____ 4. _____ 5. _____

Stunt Puzzler 3

Whoops! Nobody can find the fire extinguisher! If only one of the statements is true, where is it?

Stunt Puzzler 4

How many tandem jumps has each made?

Stella _____   Stan _____

Stunt Puzzler 5

The longest stunt jump by a car is 49.6 m. Stella just beats it by jumping a line of 3 m wide cars. How much does she beat the record by?

Stunt Puzzler 6

Nice stunt! But isn't that the director's car they've hit? If only one of the statements is true, who was driving the pick-up?

FILM SCHOOL

stunts

The World's Most Prolific Stuntman

Which stuntman has appeared in the most movies? Well just below are seven of his favourite movie stunts of all time. How does that help you with his name? First, match the movie title with its year of release and the stunt. Next write the year's blue letter in the blue column and the stunt's orange letter in the orange column. Now you have seven groups of three letters. Write them in the spaces below; they'll spell out the stuntman's name.

___ ___ ___ ___   ___ ___ ___ ___   ___ ___ ___ ___ ___ ___

Hints: **1.** Chronological order. **2.** Alphabetical order.

Movie	↓	↓	Year	Stunt
STEAMBOAT BILL **V**			1939 **O**	Every skier's fear: skiing straight off a cliff face. Fortunately, a parachute breaks the fall. **M**
STAGECOACH **T**			1978 **T**	Catapulted from a moving chariot the actor is almost trampled but climbs back in again. **N**
BEN HUR **M**			1959 **O**	Gasp! A bungee jump down a dam wall. **G**
BUTCH CASSIDY AND THE SUNDANCE KID **R**			1969 **O**	Falling more than 100 m from a helicopter. **R**
THE SPY WHO LOVED ME **A**			1995 **N**	Dashing from their hideout two cowboys jump into a river from the top of a (very big!) cliff. **E**
HOOPER **S**			1977 **R**	A house falls down around the actor. **C**
GOLDEN EYE **O**			1928 **I**	Bullets fly. A cowboy jumps from a horse, climbs under the stagecoach and back over again. **R**

PROJECT

Spot the Stuntman/woman

A few famous actors have done their own stunt work; but not many. Why? First, it's dangerous work that should only be attempted by highly trained people. Secondly, studios don't want their highly expensive actors injured!

• **Zip your favourite action movie through to the closing credits.**

• **Note the stunt actors listed. Does the film's star have his or her own stunt double?**

• **Watch the film again. Keep an eye out for scenes where the stunt actors are used. Some giveaways: you can't see the actor's face because the action is too quick, the actor's head is turned away or the action happens too far away.**

• **Find out which actors do their own stunt work.**

Lightning Jock

Lightning Jock is GMG Productions' first ever Western. With handsome heroes, feisty cowgirls, bad guys and bagpipes, the producers feel it just has to be a hit. To ensure the film is totally authentic, GMG draw up a list of totally authentic states as suitable filming locations. But some—no, most of the states here are wrong. Completely and totally wrong. So, please, before filming starts, cross out all eight of them and leave the two that are authentically Wild West.

1. Alberta
2. Arizona
3. Colorado
4. Florida
5. Hawaii
6. Kashmir
7. Manitoba
8. Northern Territory
9. South Carolina
10. Western Australia

Genre Buster

Westerns are films about the American 'Wild West'. They are usually set in the mid 19th century in places such as Utah or Arizona. They feature cowboys, ranchers, Native Americans, outlaws and the spectacular desert scenery itself.

Great Westerns

Match a word from the left lasso with a word from the right lasso to make the title of a famous Western. (Most will make sense even if you've never heard of them!) Take the two leftover words to make the three-word title at the bottom: the title of the first Western ever made.

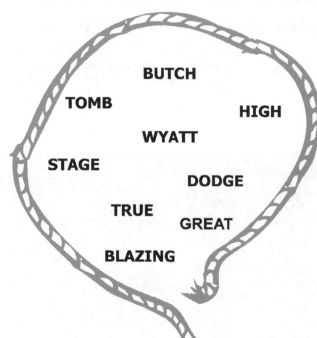

BUTCH
TOMB
HIGH
WYATT
STAGE
DODGE
TRUE
GREAT
BLAZING

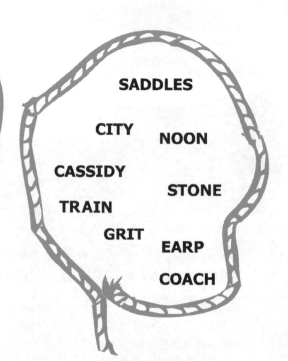

SADDLES
CITY
NOON
CASSIDY
STONE
TRAIN
GRIT
EARP
COACH

_____ _____ **ROBBERY**

Western

Poster Posers

All the answers to these puzzles are on the poster.

Anagrammaticals

The poster lists six stars. Unjumble their names to make anagrams that describe the characters they play. Use the clues and the poster to help!

Hint: Some letters have already been placed to help.

1. 'BABY' A DUCKLING
Naughty man who wears ebony

B ___ ___   G ___ ___   IN

B ___ ___ ___ ___

2. MOSS UNDERACT
Vulgar highlander

R ___ ___ ___

S ___ ___ ___ ___ M ___ ___

3. FEB DRUMFISH
Unintelligent Officer of the Law

D ___ ___ ___

S ___ ___ ___ ___ ___ ___ ___

4. VAV BERBERA
Courageous Native American warrior

B ___ ___ ___ ___

B ___ ___ ___ ___

5. LAWGY SCISSOR
Bold female cowboy

S ___ S S ___

C ___ ___ ___ ___ ___ ___

6. ROOSTER D CLOPP
Aged miner

O ___ ___

P R ___ ___ P ___ ___ ___ ___ R

Quick Numbers

How many bullet holes are there on the poster?

Word Trivia

A composition for a bagpipe is called a port. This is one of the eight homographs of the word PORT. (Homographs are words with the same spelling but different meanings.)

63

Synopsis Search

For all you Scottish folk music buffs out there:

What is the musical range of a bagpipe?

Instructions

1. Read the short (but thrilling) synopsis of *Lightning Jock*.

2. Search for each word (of four letters or more) and cross them out.

3. When you finish you'll have a goodly number of letters left over—29 to be exact. Write these lonely letters (in order from left to right) into the spaces below.

4. Have a laugh at what passes for musical humour.

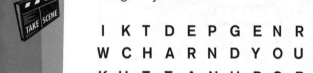

Prospector Larry Larson has struck it rich in his gold mine but hasn't counted on the Goolie Brothers Gang kidnapping his daughter Clementine for ransom. Enter Lightning Jock, a kilt-wearing artist from Scotland with a reputation for being 'quick on the draw'. The Sheriff arrests one of the outlaws for littering but the others free him and head into the desert to escape. The two heroes follow and, helped by Chief Sitting Pretty and his braves, ambush the Goolies in Really Dry Gulch for the obligatory shootout.

```
I K T D E P G E N R D B Y R R A L S O N W O L L O F H G O
W C H A R N D Y O U O C E A N T F E I H C H R O W B N J T
K U T T A N H R Q B Q T K I N K P X P D E S E R T I M J C
I R R G K J E K E W G G C R N K D G F I N T O B R O Q O X
D T R O D O F N K P N O E E E G T R K K Y C R E S Y U K W
N S I T E P B X I I U T O S P C P K A N P O T N L T J C J
A N C H P S R L R T H T C L R S S V Z W T T A G L L R I X
P T H E L T H A I G N A A Q I E O G K H I R S A C R K U Z
P D B R E C E O U G P E D T O E U R E L G T W H M Q P Q L
I C W S H W P A O E A S M R I L T R P H S S J F R G O L D
N B K G V K D Y E T C T E E C O S Y R E M B H N M W R G G
G P L O E Q D L N O O H O H L Y N J R K N R S M N K X H N
D G Y O M E K P T P D U R R L C W R R G K A U W I T H K I
R R N L M Z R L E M E D T P Y J A N J M M V B N F F T L N
D R G I R Q A F R O T Y W N N N M M W O T E M K O Z M B T
D Y M E T N N K N R N A R T I S T C Z D C S A L K S R X H
K A P S D T I P W F U F R E A L L Y N N T K K B D M R R G
D F E L W L I H W N O F F I R E H S R T L W M I N E R A I
P R R H T M K S Q N C K Y Y T T E R P P M N W T N S A H L
```

Western

Slanging Match

The West was often a wild place to live—and that was just the language! Test your knowledge of cowboy slang by matching these expressions with their meanings.

1. Look at each definition in turn.
2. Find a slang word or expression to match it and write it on the yellow line.
3. Now look at the number at the beginning of each line. Find that position letter in the slang word and write it in the circle.
4. When you finish, the circled letters will spell out a slang expression for a beginner, or inexperienced person.

buzzard food, grassed, horse feathers, loco, packin', pokey, seegar, windbagging, yellow belly

Definition		No.	
thrown by a horse	◯	1	
cigarette	◯	6	
gaol house	◯	4	
coward	◯	2	
carrying a weapon	◯	6	
ridiculous	◯	1	
crazy	◯	2	
dead	◯	6	
talking nonsense	◯	3	

STORYBOARD 1

Prospector Larry 'Gopher' Larson hits pay-dirt in his gold mine. In fact, he digs up enough gold to provide a wedding dowry for his daughter Clementine.

Picture Puzzle

Larry has carefully labelled his gold sacks with the number of nuggets they contain. Find three that add up to exactly 100.

Jumbled Director

'D HOOFN JR' is the director of the sunk-without-a-trace *Lightning Jock* movie. But rearrange the stills from the movie strip below into the correct order and you'll discover the name of a real director of Westerns—and his movies won Academy Awards! To help you, the sequence starts with the vulture.

____ _____ ___

D   H   O   O   F   N

J   R

Director Bio

I directed over 130 movies in my 45 years in filmmaking. I featured movie star John Wayne in over 20 of my movies, won Academy Awards (as best director) for four and am best known for my Westerns, which included *Stagecoach*, *Fort Apache* and *The Man Who Shot Liberty Valance*. I was the first person to ever receive an American Film Institute Life Achievement Award.

STORYBOARD 2

The Goolie Brothers rob Larry and kidnap his daughter Clementine!

Picture Puzzle

Change GOLD into CASH in four moves. Each word has one letter different from the word above and the letters can be rearranged.

G	O	L	D
Dutch shoe			
Wooden gears			
Pigs			
Cut an arm or leg			
C	A	S	H

Western

Hollywood Crossquiz

It's your next Hollywood Crossquiz and this time we can only 'oo'—not 'ah'. Read the clues and fill in the blanks. With the first letter and those two 'o's; it's almost too easy.

clue	answer
pointed weapon used in whaling	H _ _ _ O O _
in the open air	O _ _ _ O O _
crazy	L O O _ _
make fun of	L _ _ _ O O _
unruly person	Y _ _ O O _
American word for a toilet	W _ _ _ O O _
point of view	O _ _ _ O O _
strange appearance	O _ _ O O _ _
moving barrier to close an entrance	D O O _

Drinks are on the House

The barkeeper in the saloon is adding up the sarsaparilla drink totals for the past fortnight. But where the numbers were are just coloured stains. Luckily, each coloured stain stands for the same number and the bartender remembers that there's a 0, 1 and 9. So help the barkeeper out and complete the calculation.

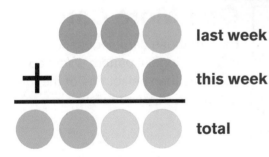

last week

+ this week

total

STORYBOARD 3

Larry heads into Duck City's saloon for a thirst—quenching sarsaparilla.

Picture Puzzle

The saloon is a square building with absolutely identical sides, the four doors certainly help with quick exits during fights.

(a) How many windows does the saloon have? _____

(b) How many verandah posts does it have? _____

Card Sharp

Duck City's resident cardsharp Jim 'Aces High' Dougherty is in the middle of a card game in the saloon.

1. If picture cards (kings, queens and jacks) are worth ten and all other cards are worth face value, which hand is worth the most?

2. If this was a poker game, who would have the best hand?

3. Jim's slipped an extra card into the pack. What is the card and which two hands have the duplicates?

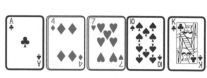

One More Card

Each of these card sequences follows a logical pattern. Work out what it is then select one of the four numbered cards to follow.

STORYBOARD 4

In the saloon Larry meets Jock, an artist (and musician) on a painting tour of the Old West. Could Jock help Larry retrieve the gold and his daughter? For a share of the gold and a free drink Jock will help anyone!

Picture Puzzle

What will the next number on Jock's bagpipes be?

Hint: The numbers in Jock's name are 10-15-3-11.

Western

Movie Matrix

Use the clues and the given letter to complete the movie matrix. When completed, one of the columns will answer this question:

What Are We?

Consisting of staggered treads and risers, cowboys (and cowgirls) often fall down us during fights.

small rodent

compass direction

to do with the navy

once more

breathe heavily while sleeping

M				
	O			
		V		
			I	
				E

Western Trivia

Stagecoaches were popular props for Westerns. Films with 'Stagecoach' in the title include *Stagecoach to Fury*, *The Last Stagecoach West*, *Stagecoach Buckaroo* and *Stagecoach Kid*.

Gunning for a Word

Despite being in a wild town Jock has said no to a gun—'Hoots mon! I'll blast 'em with me bagpipe'.

Nevertheless, here are three definitions for three words that all have the three-letter word 'GUN' in them. The missing letters, if you please.

GUN . greasy mess

. . GUN started

. . . GUN . . deep red

STORYBOARD 5

Jock needs some real Western gear so Larry sets him up with cowboy boots, a cowboy hat and a cowboy scarf. Jock insists, however, that the kilt stays.

Picture Puzzle

Jock needs a pair of boots from the shelf. Find the pair that matches.

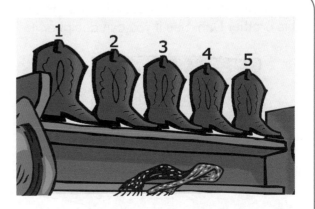

In Gaol for a Spell

Being in the Wild West, Dan Goolie was locked in a JAIL. In Australia he would have ended up in a GAOL. The box has a selection of twenty words with both their Australian and American spellings. Round them up and write them in the correct horseshoe.

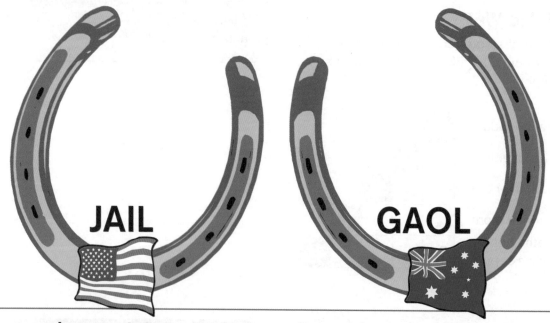

JAIL **GAOL**

pyjamas defense favorite pajamas tyre colour centre
catalogue memorise tire catalog favourite plough
center theater color plow defence theatre memorize

STORYBOARD 6

The sheriff is guarding the jail where he's locked up Dan Goolie for rustling—and that's so noisy when you're watching a movie!

Picture Puzzle

Brett Goolie has sent a coded message to his brother Dan. See if you can decipher it.

Dear Dan, we'll free you from the (!)(6)(?)(#) tonight.
(#)(?)(−)(6) has sent you a key in the (&)(6)(?)(#) today.
It's inside the (−)(6)(#)(6)(&)(?).
When you escape, meet us at the (−)(6)(≠)(−)(&)(?)(#)(#).

Western

Tee-Hee: a Teepee!

There aren't that many words with two pairs of Es in them. There's um, teepee* … and gee-gee … and—heck, use the clues to fill in the letters of these six.

*Some countries spell it tepee. We're not, otherwise this puzzle wouldn't work.

insulting term for small person	▢ ee ▢ ee
child's name for a horse	▢ ee ▢ ee
rubber cleaning implement	▢ ▢ ▢ ee ▢ ee
largest bee in a hive	▢ ▢ ee ▢ — ▢ ee
Alice in Wonderland character	▢ ▢ ee ▢ ▢ ▢ ee

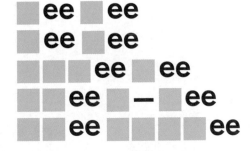

Good Intent

Here are three of Chief Sitting Pretty's teepees. By looking carefully at their size, position and colour, decide which of the six maps is the most accurate.

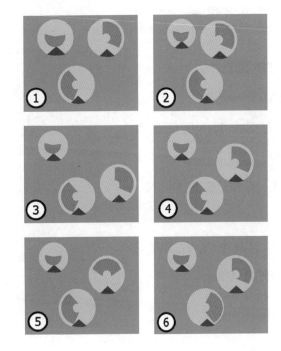

STORYBOARD 7

Larry and Jock go to visit Chief Sitting Pretty. They ask the squaw for directions to his tent.

Picture Puzzle

The squaw isn't much help. She just tells the two men he's in the odd-tent-out. But which one is that?

Go West!

Larry and Jock head into the desert to find the Indian Village. Follow their trek to see which of the four locations is Chief Sitting Pretty's village.

1. Start at the saloon.
2. Follow each direction by drawing a line from the centre of one square to the centre of the next.
3. There are two breaks along the way. Write down what you see on the map at each location.

Directions

START: saloon

N, W, SW, N, NE, N, E, N,

NW _____

N, E, N, SE, E, S, SE, N

_____

N, N, NW, NW, W, SW, S

FINISH: Village

STORYBOARD 8

Jock and Larry follow the Goolie Brothers' tracks out into the burning desert. Soon they lose their way. Above, a vulture looks hungrily down.

Picture Puzzle

Jock and Larry's path adds up to exactly 50. Which one is it: black, red or blue?

What's My Job?

Rearrange the letters in the grid to spell out this job title. Use each of the yellow square letters twice.

S	E	C
R		N
T	A	I

I paint the background sets and scenery. I make sure landscapes, buildings and signs look realistic and fit the time period.

___ ___ ___ ___ ___ ___ ___ ___ ___ ___ ___ ___

Wagon Wheelies

Four broken wagon wheels, lying in the hot sun. They're easy to fix though; just supply the missing letter (or letters as the case may be) to complete each sequence.

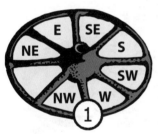

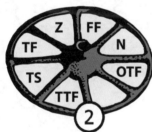

Hints:

1. The Wild West **2.** Forty-five **3.** 1, 2, 3… **4.** What shapes are wheels?

STORYBOARD 9

Fortunately a passing cart picks up the two heroes and carries them back to Duck City.

Picture Puzzle

The journey back is very slow. Jock passes the time counting the wheels turn around. If he counts 1000 revolutions, how far was it (approximately) back to Duck City?

(a) 1.6 km **(b)** 3.8 km **(c)** 5.0 km **(d)** 5.9 km   **Hint:** 1000 m = 1 km

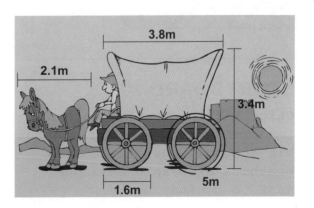

Quick Count

How many arrows in the hat?

Smoke Signals

Hidden in this smoke message are seven objects or people you might find in or around a Native American village. To find them, start from the A at the top and wind your way, one letter at a time (either vertically or horizontally) around the smoke. To make it a little easier, each word has five letters.

Western Trivia

The actor John Wayne appeared in over 250 movies (many of them Westerns). He was the leading man 142 times, and even had a US postage stamp printed in his honour. A remarkable career for a man christened Marion!

STORYBOARD 10

Chief Sitting Pretty sends an important message to Larry about his daughter. But the Goolie Brothers also send messages, just to confuse Larry.

Picture Puzzle

Only one of the four smoke signals is in the correct order. Which one is it?

Western

A

B

Desert Trek

You can easily wander around in a desert with absolutely no idea of where you're going. Fortunately for you, it doesn't really matter which way you head into this desert. You can start at A or B. Each path has its own set of clues but the same answers (just back to front). So grab a drink, your hat and the sun cream and head right in.

Path A Clues

(a) Hole in the earth from which ore is removed. (4)

(b) Animal excrement. (4)

(c) Weapon that fires bullets. (3)

(d) Thrust at with a knife. (4)

(e) Not rich. (4)

(f) To pull a gun from a holster. (4)

(g) Large carnivore, related to the dog. Hunts in packs. (4)

(h) Mineral spring. (3)

(i) Examination in court. (5)

Path B Clues

(a) Animal den. (4)

(b) Faucets. (4)

(c) Move freely. (4)

(d) Armed fight between two or more groups. (3)

(e) Hang down. (5)

(f) Flying mammal. (3)

(g) Cosy, comfortable. (4)

(h) Large African antelope. (3)

(i) Cotton cloth used for making jeans. (5)

Western

Your Place or Mine?

Here's a map of Larry's 'Last Chance' mine. All you have to do is work out which pairs of **mine** entrances connect together. So:

1. Pick a word from the word list.

2. Decide which category — cowboy equipment, horse breed, mining word, cowboy clothing, desert feature, blacksmith equipment — it fits in.

3. Draw the category tunnel shape in the matching square on the map.

Example:

Word 7 is 'shaft'. A shaft is a vertical passage into a mine. So the mine shape (C) has been drawn into square 7.

Hints: Use the tunnel sections you've completed to help with words you're not too sure about. You could even use a dictionary!

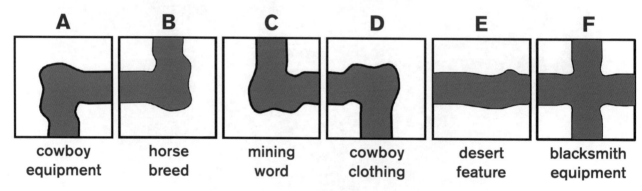

A	B	C	D	E	F
cowboy equipment	horse breed	mining word	cowboy clothing	desert feature	blacksmith equipment

Word List

1. LARIAT
2. APPALOOSA
3. REVOLVER
4. MUSTANG
5. UNDERCUT
6. CHAPS
7. SHAFT
8. SALT LAKE
9. CANTEEN
10. ANVIL
11. BUTTE
12. KERCHIEF
13. PAINT
14. SKIP
15. JEANS
16. ORE

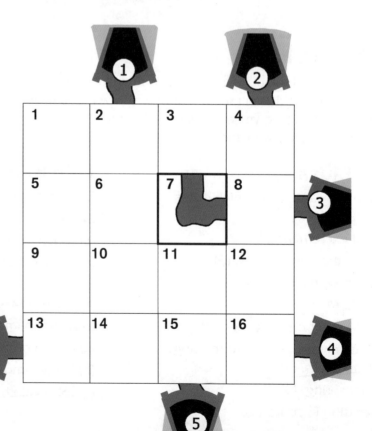

Western

Horse Tales

The horses of Lightning Jock, Clementine, Dan Goolie and the Sheriff are all different heights, have different names and enjoy eating different treats (some of which are not very healthy for working horses!)

Use the information provided and the grid to match the four characters and their horses.

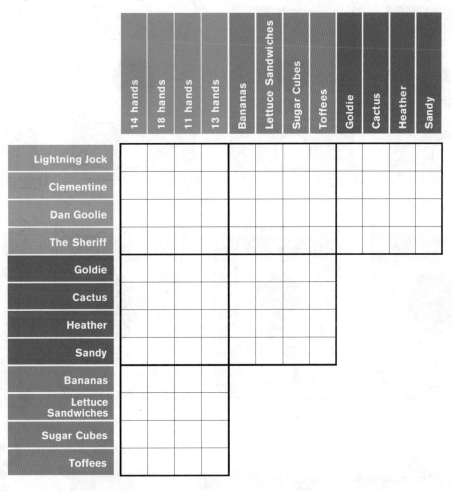

1. Lightning Jock's horse stables with Goldie, who is just one hand taller.

2. The Sheriff has trouble buying fruit for his horse, who being the tallest eats a lot.

3. The horse that loves lettuce sandwiches is named after a desert plant. She's also the shortest.

4. Clementine keeps sugar cubes in her pocket for her horse. She sometimes gives Heather some when her owner isn't in the stable.

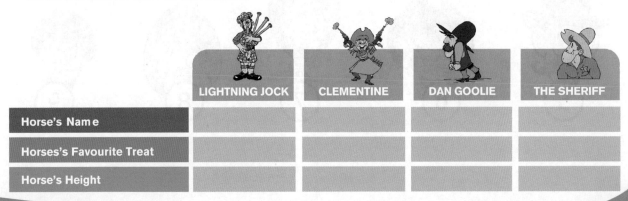

	LIGHTNING JOCK	CLEMENTINE	DAN GOOLIE	THE SHERIFF
Horse's Name				
Horses's Favourite Treat				
Horse's Height				

Wanted: Better Wanted Posters

The Duck City Wanted posters leave a lot to be desired. How can anyone spot these dastardly outlaws from just their silhouette? See how you go: check out the nine law-abiding citizens below and match eight of them to their posters. Who isn't wanted?

Western

The Lightning Jock® Trivia Quiz

In the Wild West they used to shoot first and ask questions later. We're sorry to say, but it's now later. So here come the questions. Yep pardner, ten gut-wrenching, stomach-twisting, liver-curdling questions.

Instructions

How can we put this? It's like they say in those cowboy shootouts — Draw! Except in this case it's Answer!

1. On the poster, how does Larry protect himself?
   - **(a)** With bullet-proof glass
   - **(b)** With a baseball bat
   - **(c)** With dignity
   - **(d)** With a pan

2. How many pipes are on Jock's bagpipes?
   - **(a)** Seven
   - **(b)** Five
   - **(c)** Three
   - **(d)** Two of the above

3. What type of drinks does the bartender have to tally?
   - **(a)** Whisky
   - **(b)** Diet Coke®
   - **(c)** Orange Slushees
   - **(d)** Sarsaparilla

4. What is the name of the saloon's cardsharp?
   - **(a)** Read 'em and Weep
   - **(b)** Six Card Sal
   - **(c)** Handy Andy
   - **(d)** Aces High

5. The Indian Chief is named
   - **(a)** Bison Beef
   - **(b)** Arrow There
   - **(c)** Chief
   - **(d)** Sitting Pretty

6. What bird of prey is on the trail?
   - **(a)** A condor
   - **(b)** An eagle
   - **(c)** A kookaburra
   - **(d)** A vulture

7. The town in the movie is called
   - **(a)** Dodge City
   - **(b)** Evade City
   - **(c)** Avoid City
   - **(d)** Duck City

8. Larry's Gold Mine was the
   - **(a)** Third Chance Mine
   - **(b)** Second Chance Mine
   - **(c)** No Chance Mine
   - **(d)** Last Chance Mine

9. What piece of clothing did Jock refuse to change?
   - **(a)** His jocks
   - **(b)** His undervest
   - **(c)** His tam o'shanter
   - **(d)** His kilt

10. Which direction is the river from the township?
    - **(a)** Forwards
    - **(b)** Backwards
    - **(c)** Sideways
    - **(d)** Up

Learning More

FILMS

Check these out at www.imdb.com

Stagecoach, Butch Cassidy and the Sundance Kid, Back to the Future III

COWBOY CLIPART

clipart.us.com

www.clipart.us.com/cowboy_clipart.shtml

THE WILD WEST

Cyber Soup's The Wild West www.thewildwest.org

A Wild West Party www.activitiesforkids.com/birthday/themes/west.htm

The American West www.americanwest.com

More Cowboy activities www.dltk-kids.com/crafts/miscellaneous/wildwest.htm

BAGPIPES

The Universe of Bagpipes www.hotpipes.com

Bagpipes At Best (bagpipe tunes) www.bagpipesatbest.com

Film Classification

Films are classified to give viewers an idea of their suitability for different ages. Here in Australia we have, for example, G for General exhibition and PG for Parental Guidance recommended.

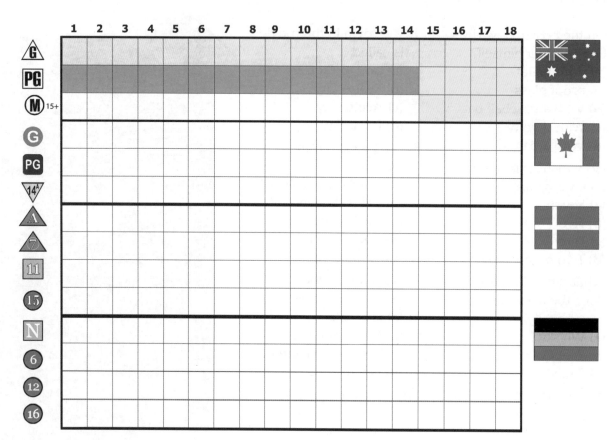

World Ratings

Different countries have different film classification systems. Complete the chart using the information below. Use two colours for ratings that require an adult up to a certain age (such as PG). Use the Australian ratings as a guide.

Canada

G: All ages

PG: All ages but parental guidance suggested for children under 8

14A: Anyone under 14 must be accompanied by an adult

Denmark

A: All ages

7: Not recommended for under 7s

11: Recommended for 11 and older

15: Recommended for 15 and older

Germany

N: No age limit

6: No one under 6 admitted

12: People aged 12 and over admitted (or between 6 and 11 with an adult)

16: No one under 16 admitted

FILM SCHOOL
film classification

What's My Classification?

How suitable are these films for different ages?
Write a classification next to each movie.
Use the codes G, PG and M15+.

 G General exhibition

 PG Parental guidance recommended for children under 15

 M15+ Mature: recommended for ages 15 and older

Star Wars ◯

Lord of the Rings: The Fellowship of the Ring ◯

Shrek ◯

Spy Kids 3D ◯

Harry Potter and the Philosopher's Stone ◯

Gone in 60 Seconds ◯

The Wizard of Oz ◯

The Princess Diaries ◯

Grease ◯

Charlie's Angels (Full Throttle) ◯

 PROJECT

R for Rating

It's high time movies had a quality rating; and it's your job to invent it! Create symbols to fit the shapes below that could be used to rate a movie. You could use existing symbols: for example, PG could mean 'pretty good' or you could make up your own; perhaps DWYM for 'Don't Waste Your Money'. Use the space below each symbol to write its meaning.

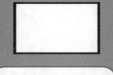  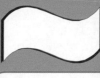

Elf Guard and the Teapot of Doom

GMG has finally convinced in-demand movie maker Jean Sprocket to direct a fantasy movie for them. *Elf Guard: the Teapot of Doom* is the result. The phenomenally successful *Elf Guard* books are read (and loved) by millions of children worldwide so GMG sees the film as a sure-fire winner. But will the readers agree?

Elf Guard: the Book

Unfortunately for fans of the books, the director has made changes to the plot, the characters and even the teapot of doom. Read the descriptions (from the book) then use the poster on page 83 to find five changes.

- **A'sthma:** a ferocious giant red dragon who lives on Black Mountain.

- **Jocular:** the evil jester who steals the teapot. She carries an enchanted talking replica of her own head on a stick.

- **Purtle:** the Elf Guard captain. Renowned for her musical skills, she commands her crack Elf Guards with a magical conch shell horn, reputedly from Atlantis.

- **Pixle:** the Elf Guard's comic relief. Tall (for an elf), he towers over the other elves and is always bumbling into trouble.

- **The Teapot of Doom:** A beautiful porcelain creation depicting a unicorn in flight.

Genre Buster

Fantasy films feature imaginary worlds, magical creatures and mythical stories. Plots often centre on quests or challenges and characters include dragons, wizards and elves. Many films have been based on Greek and Roman myths (such as that of Hercules). The worlds created by the *Lord of the Rings* author J R R Tolkien have also been influential.

Black Mountain Castle

The dreaded Black Mountain Castle is much nicer to look at when not viewed in silhouette against a burning sky. Which of the six castles is the one from the poster?

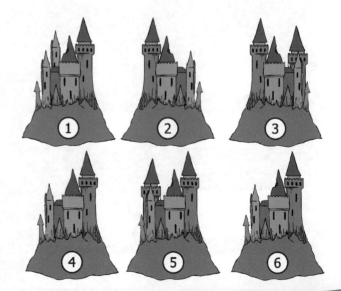

Fantasy

Poster Posers

Anagrammaticals

The poster lists four stars. Unjumble their names to make anagrams of fantasy films.

1. RENTOR GOLDFISH

A small elf-like creature has to return a band of enchanted gold to a fiery volcano.

— — — — — — — — — — — —

— — — — —

2. PERRY THROAT

A young boy is enrolled in a school for wizards.

— — — — — — — — — —

3. FIZZ HEARTWOOD

A young girl with ruby slippers joins a scarecrow, lion and tin-man on a journey along a golden road.

— — — — — — — — — — — —

— — — — — —

4. WIS WHISKERS

An ogre has to free a princess to win back his swamp. (Take the Wis from the Whiskers!)

— — — — —

5. Did you notice where the film was shot? Rearrange the title RINDL, NEW CALEDONIA to reveal the title of a well-known children's fantasy book. The book, whose characters include a small girl, a white rabbit and a Cheshire cat, has been made into movies, cartoons and a TV series!

— — — — — — — — —

— — — — — — — —

Synopsis Search

The Elf Inspector is preparing a report on the Elf Guard. After a vigorous physical, what did she write?

'The entire group is:

_____ _____ _____ _____, _____ _____ _____ _____ _____ _____ _____ _____ _____ _____ _____ _____ _____ _____

To find out:

1. Read this short and often punnish synopsis of the *Elf Guard: the Teapot of Doom*® movie.

2. Search for each word (of four letters or more) and (as you've done before), cross them out.

3. When you finish you'll have a number of letters left over (some more useful than others). Just use the first 18 and write them (in order from left to right) into the spaces above.

Elf Guard: the Teapot of Doom (Synopsis)

Catastrophe and calamity! The dread Teapot of Doom is stolen from right underneath the collective noses of Captain Purtle and the High Queen's Elf Patrol. In disgrace, the group is reassigned to the lowly border patrol post in the Outer Counties. But just for once Private Pixle has a clue. So it's not long before the Wizard Prankz and the Fort Knight have joined them on a dangerous quest to the distant Black Mountain Castle. Will the heroes survive a night in the Dreadfully Dark and Damp Forest? Can they best A'sthma, the Really Raspy Red Dragon? Or is it the world's very last tea-time …

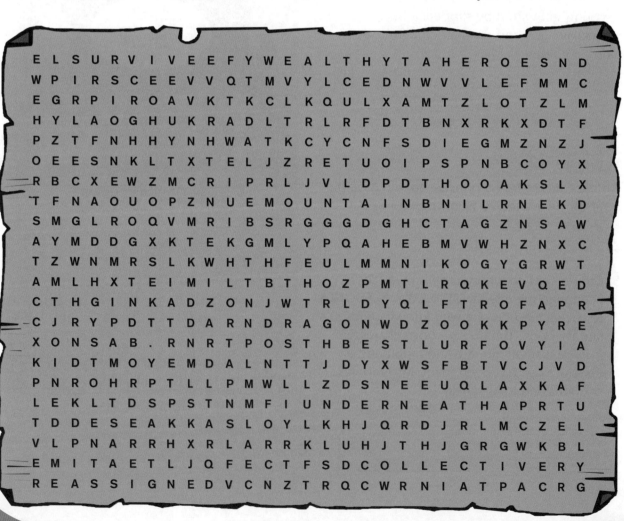

Fantasy

Jumbled Director

While **JEAN SPROCKET** might be the director of **Elf Guard** there's a much more famous director's name hidden within the scrambled letters. Rearrange the stills from the movie strip below into the correct order and you'll discover the name of the director who made all three of the **Lord of the Rings** movies.

To help you, this sequence (shot at the Wizard's Tower) starts with neither the dragon nor the (soon-to-be) Black Knight in sight.

You could also try to work out the director's name by reading his biography opposite.

____ ____ ____ ____ ____

____ ____ ____ ____ ____ ____ ____ ____ ____

Director Bio

I was born in Pukerua Bay, North Island, New Zealand in 1961.

I was given my first movie camera when I was eight and made films with my friends.

I once had to make latex models for a movie, so I used my mum's oven; I liked the movie *King Kong* so much I cut up her fur coat to make a model of the monster!

My films include all three movies in the *Lord of the Rings* series, *King Kong* and *The Frighteners*. I also co-produced the kids' TV series *Ship to Shore*.

Oh, and I often wear shorts — even in freezing weather!

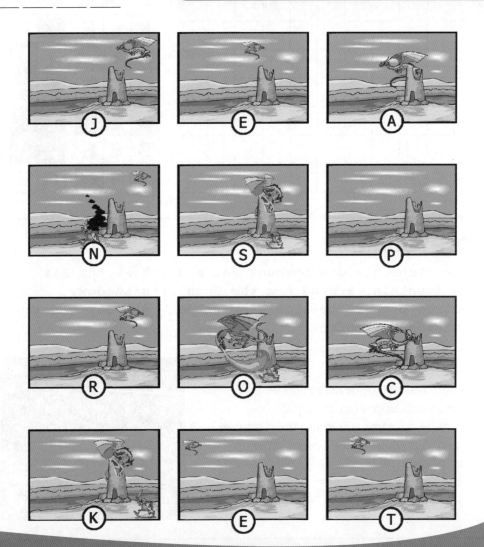

Fantasy

Crossword Scramble

This is just an ordinary little crossword puzzle. But with no clues. And the answers are filled in. Oh, and it's been cut up into 16 pieces. And scrambled. So, now you mention it, this really isn't an ordinary little crossword puzzle. It looks a little tricky but:

1. You've seen most of these words before.

2. The coloured backgrounds are a BIG clue.

3. One section has already been drawn in.

4. Jocular (the evil jester) has hidden the Teapot of Doom somewhere in the puzzle (though not very well).

STORYBOARD 1

```
Pixle stops his dragonmount for a drink at the Elf
Home fountain. Around him the Jocular's shadowy
spectres prepare to steal the teapot, already glowing
in unheeded warning.
```

Picture Puzzle

Spectres are ghostlike creatures whose shadows only appear in starlight.
How many spectres are in the town square?
Oh, and just where is the teapot glowing (in unheeded warning)?

Magic Spells

Magic spells can be as easy as 1-2-3 (insert magic word), especially if you're turning, say, GOLD into a TACO. But they can also be as difficult as 1-2-3-4 or even 1-2-3-4-5. Test your magic spelling by turning the top word into the bottom word by following the clues and changing just one letter each time and rearranging the letters if you need to. Oh, and if you get tired—just rest for a spell…

F	R	O	G
T	O	A	D

fortified place

a lettering style

a musical symbol

having toes

G	O	L	D
T	A	C	O

wooden shoe

black fire fuel

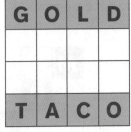

T	E	A	P	O	T
G	R	U	D	G	E

turn around

point to shoot at

roof channel that catches water

walk heavily, like through mud

Q	U	E	S	T
T	O	I	L	S

peaceful

provide with equipment

secure with ropes

flower from Holland

person who flies planes

STORYBOARD 2

Having failed to protect the Teapot of Doom, the Guards leave Elf Home in disgrace and ride straight into danger.

Picture Puzzle

Which of these four cubes can be assembled from the 'danger' net in the picture?

Movie Matrix

Use the clues and the given letter to complete the movie matrix. When completed, one of the columns will answer this question:

What Am I?

I'm a group of people who enjoy singing. I'm often found in churches or schools and I usually have a conductor and accompanist.

eat noisily

butterfly-like insects

widespread damage

upstairs room

glower

M				
	O			
		V		
			I	
				E

Fantasy Film Trivia

The elf-like creatures in *The Wizard of Oz* are called Munchkins. While filming, the Munchkins were paid $50 a week. Toto, Dorothy's dog (real name Terry) received $125 a week.

One of the Munchkins was, for a short while, the shortest pilot licensed to fly in the USA.

Monster Spotter's Guide

Are these monsters awful—or awfully nice? Each of the word strips contains a four-letter word that describes each monster's personality. Match the correct decoding bar to the word strip and that monster's personality will be revealed.

FOLMUWL   IXCEKEY   OVIRLSE   WONISCE   ESTVOIL

STORYBOARD 3

Border patrol is very boring. Nothing happens again, again and again.

Picture Puzzle

To make patrolling more interesting, the Elf Guard changes watch at regular intervals. Look at the clocks and decide when the next change of guard will happen.

Fantasy

Hop, Step, Jump

Purtle is wandering in the woods by the border crossing when she finds a pool of stepping stones. Start from one and finish at one hundred by following a simple sequence.
Hint: the answer is at your feet…

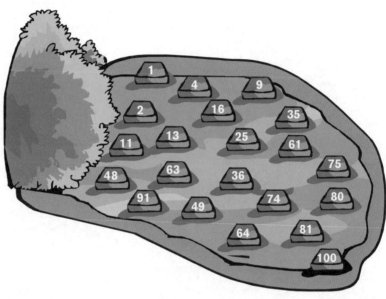

Sword in the Stone

On the other side of the stepping stones Purtle finds this strange stone with a sword embedded in it. Since you can't help her pull the sword out (after all, it's only printed on paper) be of assistance by finding the word SWORD embedded in the word STONE.

STORYBOARD 4

Private Plaits picks flowers in the forest, unaware of the danger lurking nearby.

Picture Puzzle

There are suspicious signs of silent spectators amongst the sycamore trees of the forest. Each soaring seed names a danger but where does each word start?

_____   _____

_____   _____

Fantasy

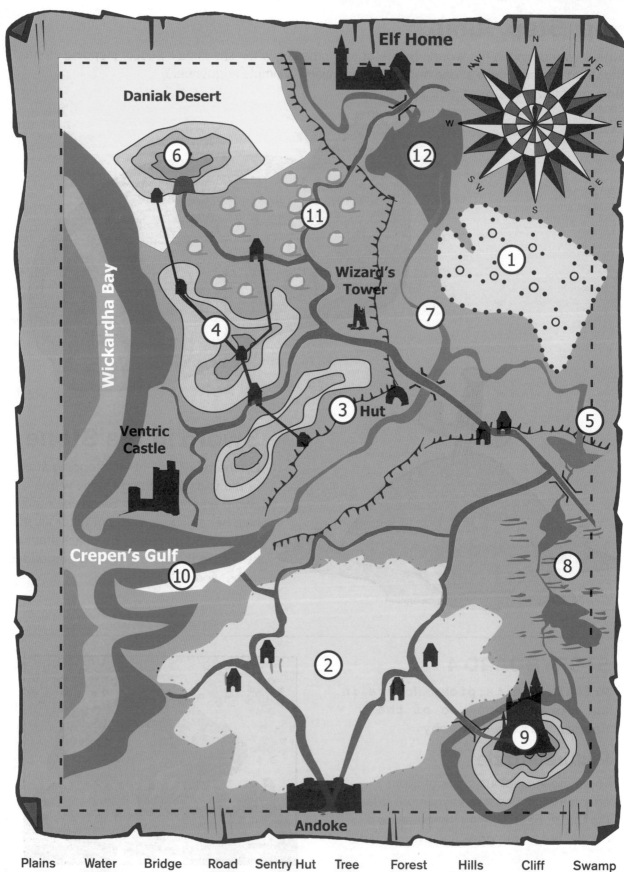

Elf Home

Daniak Desert

(6)

(12)

Wickardha Bay

(11)

Wizard's Tower

(1)

(7)

(4)

(3) Hut

Ventric Castle

(5)

Crepen's Gulf

(10)

(8)

(2)

(9)

Andoke

| Plains | Water | Bridge | Road | Sentry Hut | Tree | Forest | Hills | Cliff | Swamp |

Fantasy

The Quest Begins...

No self-respecting fantasy is complete without a detailed map of the fantasy world. So on page 90 the Elf Guard map shows a few places we've seen already, including Elf Home, the Wizard's Tower and the Border Patrol hut. First up though: use your logic, mapping and navigation skills to locate these 12 places on the map. As you find each one, write its number in. You'll need them for later.

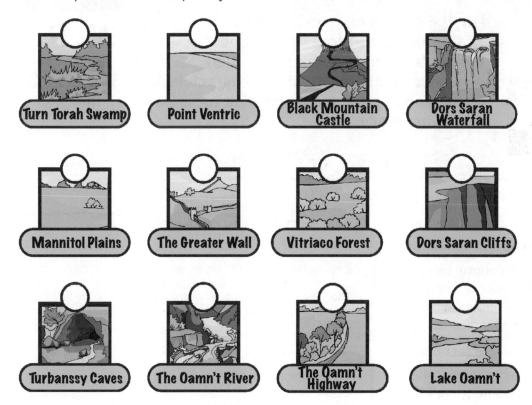

Turn Torah Swamp   Point Ventric   Black Mountain Castle   Dors Saran Waterfall

Mannitol Plains   The Greater Wall   Vitriaco Forest   Dors Saran Cliffs

Turbanssy Caves   The Oamn't River   The Oamn't Highway   Lake Oamn't

On the Road Again

Follow these descriptive passages on the map. Each has a question to answer. Once again, logic, map skills (and common sense!) will help supply an answer.

1. Leave Elf Home in disgrace. Trudge SW past the lake. Start puffing and panting. Why?

2. Continuing South down the road see a dragon flying over. Hide. On the left or right of the road?

3. Pass a fork in the road. Reach a second fork. Conclude someone is throwing out cutlery. Laugh. Get caught in violent thunderstorm. Run for cover. Where?

4. Reach the Border Patrol Hut. Relieve current patrol. Current patrol relieved to be relieved and leave in boat. Purtle stands on the bridge looking at Elf Home. She throws a stick in the water. Does it float NE or SW?

5. A few weeks later Pixle is on night duty. He sees strange lights, high in the sky. The Teapot of Doom is being used! Did the lights come from Ventric Castle, Andoke or Black Mountain Castle?

6. The Elf Guard decides to get the teapot back. They sail down the river. Where do they land?

7. They follow the road to an intersection. Why do they head north?

8. It's dark by the time they reach the next intersection. Everybody gets wet feet. Does Purtle order the patrol to travel North, South or East?

What's My Job?

Rearrange the letters in the grid to spell out this job title. Use the light pink square letters twice and the dark pink square letter three times.

E	R	C
I		T
S	W	P

I'm the person responsible for writing the film's story. I describe the film's setting, outline the action sequences and provide all the characters' dialogue. My writing is often the inspiration for making the film in the first place.

___ ___ ___ ___ ___ ___ ___   ___ ___ ___ ___ ___ ___

Screenplay

Here's part of the screenplay (script) for *Elf Guard: the Teapot of Doom*. It uses some unusual abbreviations. Find an abbreviation that means:

1. This part of the scene is set outside.

2. This part of the scene is set inside.

3. The character speaking is not on the screen.

4. The character isn't seen speaking this line but is heard like a narrator, commenting on the action.

5. A sudden jump to a different piece of action.

6. The scene will appear gradually from black.

```
FADE IN:

EXT. POINT VENTRIC, CREPEN´S GULF – NIGHT

The threatening storm has arrived. Huge
waves swamp the sailboat as lightning
stabs the sky.

EXT. SAILBOAT´S FORWARD DECK

Captain Purtle wrestles with the
ship´s wheel.

                CAPTAIN PURTLE
          Any luck Wizard?

                WIZARD PRANKZ (O.S.)
          Even my spells can't fix
          a sinking ship!

                CAPTAIN PURTLE (V.O.)
          I knew right then we
          were in for a wet and
          wild night.

CUT TO:

INT: THE SHIP´S HOLD

Private Pixle is frantically cutting the
ropes binding his panicking dragon steed.

EXT: POINT VENTRIC ROCKS

The jagged rocks are illuminated in a
flash of lightning…
```

STORYBOARD 5

The Elf Guard sail down towards Crepen's Gulf. Finding a landing spot isn't easy; towering cliffs lie between them and Black Mountain Castle.

Picture Puzzle

How tall are the cliffs? Purtle has worked out two measurements, provide the third.

You may find this knotted rope useful (or knot!)

Across the Moat

The Guard reach the castle but are stuck here at the moat. The drawbridge is up, elves don't like water and can't jump. There are however three planks conveniently lying in the shrubs. Unfortunately they're only 5 m long; the exact width of the moat. How could you place the planks so they will safely reach the other side?

Of course there is no nailing, gluing, tying or other tricks that would spoil a good puzzle.

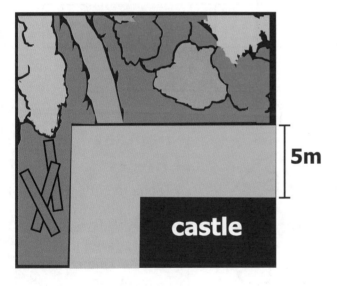

5m

castle

STORYBOARD 6

Once in the grounds the Elf Guard look for a way into the dungeons below the castle.

Picture Puzzle

Evil masterminds are usually up high (think turrets) or down low (think dungeons). So which way to go?

Decode the mysterious inscription on the door's arch for some vital information.

Hollywood Crossquiz

Oo! It's the 'oos' turn to light up Hollywood! Use the clues, fill in the blanks. As easy as, oo, saying oo.

clue	answer
plural of hoof	H O O V E S
passed in a car	O _ _ _ _ O O _
pool of water near the sea	L A G O O N
somebody who looks like somebody else	L O O K A L I K E
a book of yearly events	Y E A R B O O K
wooden wind instrument	W O O D W I N D
book for reading orders in	O _ _ _ _ O O
cook too much	O _ _ _ O O
dreadful, terrible fate	D O O M

What's Next?

No matter if you're a hobbit or a human, an elf or a wizard, you shouldn't have to go on a dangerous, death-defying quest to discover the missing letter in this sequence. Still stuck? See the Fantasy Genre Buster info, earlier on in this section.

J ? E
R I
R K
T O L

STORYBOARD 7

The Fort Knight is sent ahead to scout the castle grounds. Despite a clanking suit of armour and a tendency to bang into walls, he manages to finally reach the inner portcullis where four heavy integers lay in weight, er wait, for him ...

Picture Puzzle

To unlock the gate, place the four numbers back into their correct spots on the magic portcullis.

Fantasy

Mirror, Mirror on the Wall

Jocular, the evil jester, watches the Elf Guard in her magic mirror. 'Hah!' she cackles, 'they don't have a clue!' This magic mirror puzzle however has seven clues. As you'd expect, that means there are seven answers.

Now those seven answers all start at the numbered sections but each one overlaps the answer before and the answer after. How big an overlap? Well some share one letter, some share two letters and one even shares four letters.

Extra Hints

All the answers are to do with glass and mirrors. All the answers run clockwise around the mirror frame. The last answer ends with the first two letters of the first word. Magic!

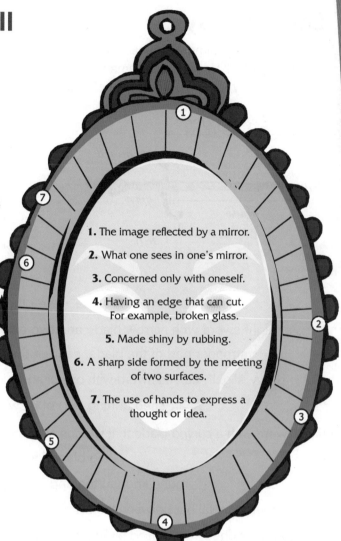

1. The image reflected by a mirror.
2. What one sees in one's mirror.
3. Concerned only with oneself.
4. Having an edge that can cut. For example, broken glass.
5. Made shiny by rubbing.
6. A sharp side formed by the meeting of two surfaces.
7. The use of hands to express a thought or idea.

STORYBOARD 8

The intrepid heroes dash about the castle, desperately searching for the Teapot of Doom. Will they find it before Jocular pours her next cuppa? Or does the Elf Guard 'have it in the bag'?

Picture Puzzle

Where is the teapot? Pick any tower.

1. Multiply the number on the tower by itself. (In other words, square it.)
2. Add 17.
3. Divide by 12.

If your answer ends in 0.5, you're looking in the wrong tower. Try again!

Sword Play

Sword fights are almost an essential part of a fantasy movie. But how well do you know your swords and their parts? Use the diagrams below to help you complete the word puzzle. The pink column will (eventually) spell out the name of a common type of sword.

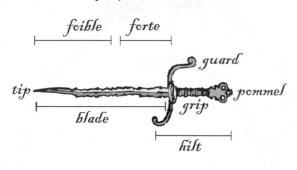

gladius rapier sabre cutlass scabbard scimitar

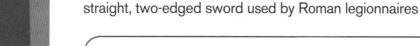

weaker part of the blade, nearer the tip

straight sword with narrow blade and two edges

stronger part of the blade, nearest the hilt

heavy, slightly curved sword with one sharp edge

sharpened cutting part of a sword

Turkish sword with a curved blade that widens near the tip

long bladed weapon

round knob at the end of the hilt

protective metal bar between the hilt and the blade

straight, two-edged sword used by Roman legionnaires

STORYBOARD 9

The throne room is guarded by a wizened old gnome with very curly toes.

Picture Puzzle

There are magic spells aplenty in the THRONE room. Rearrange the letters of THRONE to make it:

1. A STINGING INSECT __ __ __ __ __ __

2. AN ADDITIONAL ONE __ __ __ __ __ __ __ (you'll need an extra letter A)

3. TO DECREASE IN LENGTH __ __ __ __ __ __ __ (for this you'll need another S)

4. IN THE NORTH __ __ __ __ __ __ __ __ (use the extra letters N and R)

5. IN THE SOUTH __ __ __ __ __ __ __ __ (use the extra letters S and U)

Fantasy

Teapot of Double

Follow our handy-dandy Teapot-of-Doom spotter's guide and select the real Teapot from this collection of twelve look-a-likes.

The Teapot of Doom® — lid, spout, handle

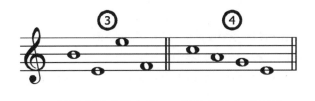

Song for A'sthma

In Storyboard 10 Pixle plays one of these four tunes to charm A'sthma, the fire-breathing dragon.

Use the note-names chart to decode each tune, then decide which of the four would appeal most to a hungry, giant, purple dragon.

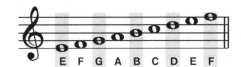

E F G A B C D E F

STORYBOARD 10

Out on the turrets Purtle fights the giant dragon A'sthma with her trusty hunting horn.

Picture Puzzle

Look at the picture. How tall do you think A'sthma is? A clue: she's between 2 and 9 dragemes.* To check your answer:

1. Multiply your guess (between 2 and 9) by 12,345,679**

2. Multiply your answer by 9

3. If you see your number then you've guessed correctly!

* An ancient measure of dragon length. One drageme is equal to approximately ten metres (1 dr = 10 m)
** Yes, a calculator would be handy.

Rotten Monsters

El Pongo, Mal'Odour, Niff and Stench are four smelly monsters who live on Black Mountain. They all have distinctive smells, have each bathed a different number of times in their lives and all are mortally afraid of a single item (of a cleansing nature). Use the information provided to match the monsters with their aromas, bath-tallies and the item they're afraid of. Remember that in logic puzzles knowing something isn't true is just as useful as finding something that is true.

	0	1	2	365	perfume	soap	deodorant	scrubbing brush	dirty socks	rotting garbage	sneakers	banana skins
Stench												
Mal'Odour												
El Pongo												
Niff												
dirty socks												
rotting garbage												
sneakers												
banana skins												
perfume												
soap												
deodorant												
scrubbing brush												

Information

1. Niff has had less baths than Mal'Odour. He's been scared of soap ever since his mother washed his mouth out for using the 'B' word* when he was in the bath.

2. Stench was once bailed up by a knight armed with a can of deodorant. He escaped by hiding in a second-hand shoe shop.

3. El Pongo has had more baths than Mal'Odour. One of them occurred when a short-sighted giant ape mistook him for a banana and dunked him in a vat of cream to make a banana split. To make his day even worse, the monster who smells of rotting garbage cleaned him up with a horrible scrubbing brush.

4. Mal'Odour had a narrow escape when he was picked up by the garbage collectors (looks like a garbage bag, smells like a garbage bag...).

*Bath

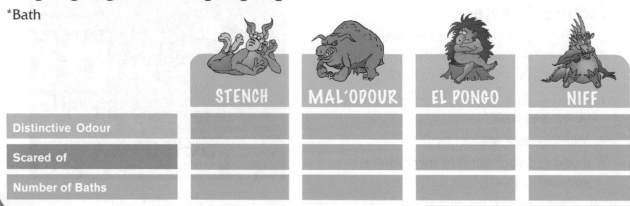

	STENCH	MAL'ODOUR	EL PONGO	NIFF
Distinctive Odour				
Scared of				
Number of Baths				

Fantasy

The Great Elf Guard Trivia Quiz

When J R R Tolkien was busy inventing Middle Earth (the setting for the *Lord of the Rings*) he didn't just create the characters and a few places for them to visit. No siree no. He invented a complete history, spoken and written languages, fauna, flora and even the phases of the moon. So, in keeping with that great tradition, here is the Elf Guard trivia quiz.

Instructions

Let's see. Read the questions, answer the questions, check the answers?

1. Where is Captain Purtle's horn reputed to have come from?
   (a) Atlantis
   (b) Atlanta
   (c) The Atlantic
   (d) An old Holden

2. What was the name of the Wizard who accompanied the Elf Guard on their quest?
   (a) Wizard Prankz
   (b) Wizard Idea
   (c) Kitchen Wiz
   (d) Wizard Home Loans

3. What colour dragon turned the Fort Knight into the Blackened Knight?
   (a) Blue
   (b) Brown
   (c) Beige
   (d) Bronze

4. What ornamental feature is in the centre of Elf Home's town square?
   (a) A fountain
   (b) A statue
   (c) A band stand
   (d) A wishing well

5. Which of the elf guards picked flowers in the forest?
   (a) Private Plaits
   (b) Private Party
   (c) Private Patient
   (d) Private School

6. Wickardha Bay is:
   (a) South-west of Elf Home
   (b) East of Eden
   (c) North of Alaska
   (d) A great fishing spot

7. What was Pixle doing in the ship's hold during the storm?
   (a) Freeing his dragonmount
   (b) Taking swimming lessons
   (c) Being sick
   (d) Cutting a hole to let the water out of the boat

8. In what way were the throne room guard's shoes unusual?
   (a) They were red and curly
   (b) They were blue and smelly
   (c) They were made from pixie dust and dreams
   (d) They were actually quite stylish

9. What gender is the evil jester Jocular?
   (a) Female
   (b) Male
   (c) See question (a)
   (d) See question (b)

10. What did Captain Purtle pull out of the rock in the forest?
    (a) A sword
    (b) A splinter
    (c) A rabbit
    (d) A particularly nice specimen of conglomerate

Learning More

FILMS

Lord of the Rings official site
www.lordoftherings.net

Wizard of Oz official site
thewizardofoz.warnerbros.com

BOOKS

Lord of the Rings
www.tolkienonline.com

Funny fantasy: Terry Pratchett
www.heartoglory.com/fantasy/pratchett-children.htm

ELVES AND DRAGONS

A Short History of Elves
news.nationalgeographic.com/kids/2003/12/elves.html

PBS Dragon Tales
pbskids.org/dragontales

MISCELLANEOUS

Totally Teapots
www.totallyteapots.com

Online Magic Squares
www.allmath.com

Maps
www.nationalgeographic.com/maps

Cinema General Knowledge

Test your cinema general knowledge with this all-singing, all-dancing word puzzle!

Read each clue then pick the word (or words) to fit that puzzle position. When finished the letters in the pale pink squares will spell out the name of a popular type of cinema that started in the USA in 1905. The dark pink squares are blank squares.

1. Outdoor cinema for cars.

2. Price of first theatre tickets.

3. Expression used to describe films or cinemas.

4. Piece of paper used for admittance into a theatre.

5. A cinema with more than one screen.

6. A cinema with more than twenty screens.

7. Piece of equipment used to shine the film image on a screen.

8. Sound system that uses multiple speakers placed around an audience.

9. Line used to queue cinema goers before entering the theatre.

10. Musical instrument used to accompany early films.

11. Name of oldest and largest cinema chain in Australia.

Word List

cents, drive, five, greater, holding, in, line, Megaplex, multiplex, piano, projector, screen, silver, sound, surround, ticket, union

What's a Cinema?

Well, a cinema is a 'movie hall' and comes from the French word 'cinéma' which is a shortened version of the word 'cinématographe' which was invented by two French film makers in the 1890s who used the Greek word that means 'movement'. And that Greek word was what? Put this flashing sign into the correct order and find out. (It flashes in a clockwise direction.)

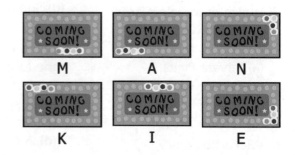

FILM SCHOOL

cinemas

Screen Aspect Ratios

Yes, it sounds technical but screen aspect ratio simply means; how does the width of a movie screen compare to its height? Normal TVs are set at 'Academy Standard': the width is 1.33 times the height. 'Cinemascope' has a much larger aspect ratio: the width is 2.35 times the height.

How Big?

Work out these screen sizes. A calculator might be handy! Round the answers off to one decimal point.

1. How wide is a 3 m high ACADEMY STANDARD screen? _____

2. How high is a 7.4 m wide ACADEMY FLAT screen? _____

3. How wide is a 4.5 m high CINEMASCOPE screen? _____

2.35 into 1.33 doesn't go…

Look at the original Cinemascope (2.35 X 1) film on the left. Which of the three pictures on the right show how it would look on an Academy Standard (1.33 X 1) size TV screen?

PROJECT

Do-it-yourself Cinemascope

You can use a photo-editing program (such as Paint) to create 'Cinemascope'-sized pictures from your own photographs.

1. Open a copy of an interesting photograph in your photo-editing program.

2. Determine how wide the picture is. In Paint, click on the Image menu then click on Attributes. The dialog box will tell you the height and width.

3. Use the select tool to select an area that is 2.35 times wider than it is high. For example, if your photograph is 800 pixels wide a selection 340 pixels high would create a Cinemascope-sized area.

4. Copy the selection. Create a new file. Paste the selection.

MINT SPIES: AFTERBURN

Mint Spies: Afterburn is GMG Productions' newest action movie. The all original story features three female spies who work at the Australian Mint and their boss Ray-Son. Their job: keep the country's billions secure, hunt down enemy agents and protect the nation's piggy-banks.

Licensed to Make Money

The James Bond spy/action movies (originally written by author Ian Fleming) are one of the highest grossing series of all time. To find out which of these five James Bond films made the most* money:

1. Fill in the missing letters of the five films below.

2. Each missing letter is the initial letter of a colour in the maze. Write in the five colours.

3. Start in the first row with the first colour, then move through the maze in the same order as the colours.

4. Keep repeating the sequence of colours until you reach the bottom row.

5. Your last colour matches the highest grossing film.

*After adjusting for the fact that money isn't worth as much as it used to be!

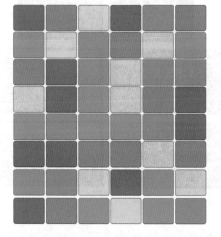

MOVIE	COLOUR
DIE ANOTHE__ DAY	
G__LDEN EYE	
THE SP__ WHO LOVED ME	
THUNDER __ALL	
__OLDFINGER	

Action Film Trivia

In the film *Mission Impossible* Tom Cruise had to hang on to steel cables above a vault floor. In the actual filming he kept hitting his head on the floor until he balanced himself with coins in his shoes.

Genre Buster

Action films have lots of – wait for it – action! They feature dangerous stunts, chases, gun-play, fights, explosions, disasters and special effects. They often focus on a hero and sidekick or a group of adventurers fighting together. Action films often combine genres with science fiction, Westerns, horror, war or as in the case of *The Spy Was a Chair*, stupidity…

Action

Poster Posers

All the answers to these puzzles are on the poster.

Anagrammaticals

The poster lists four stars. Unjumble their names to make anagrams that mean:

1. REN SLICE

Device to muffle the noise of a gun.

S i l e n c e r ✓

2. DOT MORIC

A tiny photograph, as small as the head of a pin.

M _ _ _ _ _ _ _ _

3. DI GUSSIE

Something worn to change a person's appearance.

D i s g u i s e

4. DEZ NERVOUS

A meeting at a certain time or place.

R _ _ _ _ _ _ _ _ _ _ _

Hint: The first letters have already been placed to help.

Quick Numbers

How many issues (combined) do the three publications listed on the poster put out each (non-leap) year?

428   429   430   431

Word Trivia

The word 'spy' comes from the old Latin word 'specere', which means 'to look'. Related 'looking' words include spectator, spectacles, inspect and inspector.

"NUT-MEG"
REN SLICE

"BRANDY"
DOT MORIC

"CINNA-MON"
DI GUSSIE

"RAY-SON"
DEZ NERVOUS

Four mint spies...
Two dangerous foes...
One huge movie!

"Spicy!"
The Flavouring Daily
"Sudsy"
The Washing Weekly
"Saucy!"
Ketchup Makers Monthly

MINT SPIES
AFTERBURN

GMG PRODUCTIONS PRESENT
A GIZ ORDURE FILM • SCRIPT BY TUTTI H McKOY

Synopsis Search

It's the question on everyone's lips at headquarters.

Just why did the spy wear a blanket on her head?

— — — —   — — — —   — — —

— — — — — — — — — — — — — —

— — — — — — — — — — — —

To find out:

1. Read this short and occasionally humorous synopsis of the *Mint Spies: Afterburn®* movie.

2. Search for each word (of four letters or more) and (as you've probably done before), cross them out.

3. When you finish you'll have a stack of letters left over. But you only need the first 27 which you need to write (in order from left to right) into the spaces above.

MINT SPIES: AFTERBURN SYNOPSIS

The team's skills and underarm deodorants are put to the test when a secret organisation plots to flood Australia with inflammable counterfeit money. A bizarre robbery of printing plates and mouth fresheners from the mint is the beginning of this dangerous assignment as the girls travel the world in search of clues they could have found back in Canberra. But do the ladies possess the street smarts to thwart the evil scheme to leave a lasting after-burn in people's wallets?

Action

Beat the Bomb

Ray-Son doesn't have much time left to defuse the bomb. But how much time is not much time? There's one sure-fire way (aside from letting it explode) to learn this important information:

1. Read each question and circle the best of the two answers.

2. Look at the black segment next to your answer. Colour in the same segment on the big digital clock. For example, if you think the answer to RED DIGIT 1 is 7, then colour in the top segment of the red digit on the big clock. If you think the correct answer is 8 then colour in the middle segment.

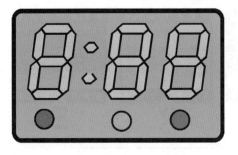

RED DIGITS

1. Wonders of the ancient world	7	8	
2. Signs of the zodiac	10	12	
3. Cards in a deck (no jokers)	48	52	
4. Known planets in the solar system	9	10	
5. Squares on a chess board	49	64	

YELLOW DIGITS

1. Keys on a piano	88	40	
2. Stars on the Australian flag	7	6	
3. Holes on a golf course	15	18	
4. A baker's dozen	12	13	
5. Santa's reindeer (including Rudolph)	9	18	

BLUE DIGITS

1. Blind mice	3	7	
2. Digits in an Australian postcode	4	5	
3. Words a picture is worth	100	1000	
4. Dalmatians	91	101	
5. Days to travel around the world	70	80	

STORYBOARD 1

Brandy is staking out a hamburger joint when she overhears two spies discussing their plan to rob the mint.

Picture Puzzle

The hamburger joint is very noisy and Brandy isn't absolutely certain about a key word she heard. Look at the five words and decide which is the odd one out before Brandy has to turn around and leave.

race car?
rail car?
re-paper?
reviver?
rotator?

TOP SECRET

Jumbled Director

'GIZ ORDURE' is the director of the not-so-well known *Mint Spies* movie. But rearrange the stills from the movie strip below into the correct order and you'll discover the name of a spy-movie director. And his films are much more famous!

To help you, the sequence starts with the spy approaching an ATM. You could also try to work out the director's name by reading his biography opposite.

ROBERT __ __ __ __ __ __ __ __ __

Director Bio

I knew I wanted to be a director when I was 12 and saw the movie *Escape from New York*.

My first major film was *El Mariachi* which I made for just $7000!

I am best known for the three *Spy Kids* films which I wrote and directed. I have nine brothers and sisters and some have acted in my films.

G   I   Z

O   R   D   U   R   E

STORYBOARD 2

Three junior spies are turned into trees and arranged decoratively in the city park to watch for enemy activity.

Picture Puzzle

Turn these two 'spy' words into new words. Working downwards, add the new letter to the letters above to create a new word. The order of the letters can be changed.

Hint: The puzzle includes words that mean a small bunch of flowers, baked dough, being nimble, carelessness, to cover with water, very wet.

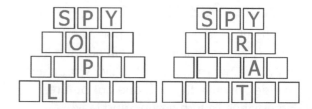

Action

Target Practice

Ray-Son, Cinna-Mon, Nut-Meg and Brandy head down to the target range for practice. Here are their targets after five shots.

Match each target to a person and calculate each score.

Clues

1. Nut-Meg was the only person to miss the target board.

2. Brandy and Cinna-Mon's scores are multiples of three.

3. Ray-Son had the smallest score.

4. Cinna-Mon was the most consistent shooter.

1 point
3 points
9 points
27 points

SCORING

STORYBOARD 3

The junior spies' vigilance pays off and the enemy's planning map is located. Mint Spy Nut-Meg breaks into the building and snaps a picture.

Picture Puzzle

Which of these four maps is the one Nut-Meg photographed?

SNAP!

MAIN MAP

A **B** **C** **D**

Location Shots

Action

On Location

Mint Spies is being filmed on location in many exciting locations around the world. Match up the 15 photos on the page opposite with the name of each famous landmark and its country.
When you finish, the coloured circles in the country names spell out the location of the final chase scene.

Landmarks

Egyptian Pyramid, Eiffel Tower, Greek ruins, El Castillo (Mayan pyramid), Machu Pichu (Incan city), Mt Everest, Niagara Falls, Samurai Castle, Statue of Liberty, Stonehenge, Sydney Opera House, Taj Mahal, Venetian canals, Dutch windmills, Temple

Countries

Australia, Canada, Egypt, United Kingdom, France, Greece, India, Italy, Japan, Mexico, Netherlands, Peru, Thailand, Tibet, USA

LANDMARK	LOCATION
1. _____	○○●○○
2. _____	○○○○●○ ○○○○○●○
3. _____	○○○○●○○○○
4. _____	●○○○○○
5. _____	○○○●
6. _____	○○○○○○○●
7. _____	○○○○
8. _____	●○○○
9. _____	●○○○
10. _____	●○○○○
11. _____	○○●
12. _____	○○○○●
13. _____	●○○○○○
14. _____	○○○○○○●○○
15. _____	●○○○○

Fly the (Right) Flag

What's the next flag in this sequence? Choose from 1, 2 or 3.

(**Hint:** Look carefully at the location photographs again.)

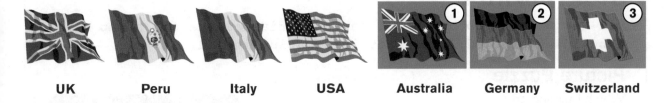

| UK | Peru | Italy | USA | Australia ① | Germany ② | Switzerland ③ |

Odd one out

Which location in each group is the odd one out?

Group 1

Egyptian pyramid, Greek ruins, Stonehenge, Mt Everest, Mayan Pyramid, Machu Pichu

Group 2

Eiffel Tower, Greek ruins, Sydney Opera House, Venetian canals, Dutch windmills

Movie Matrix

Use the clues and the given letter to complete the movie matrix. When completed, one of the columns will answer this question:

supernatural

shoreline

polite

Arab leader

untrue

M				
	O			
		V		
			I	
				E

What Am I?

I'm a small wooden hammer used to attract attention or reduce noise in formal situations. I'm often used by judges and auctioneers.

Counterfeit Notes

Quick: find at least 10 things wrong with this counterfeit Australian one dollar note!

1. _____
2. _____
3. _____
4. _____
5. _____
6. _____
7. _____
8. _____
9. _____
10. _____

Action Film Trivia

Ian Fleming, the creator of the James Bond series, also wrote the children's book *Chitty Chitty Bang Bang*.

STORYBOARD 4

Nut-Meg finds a photograph of an industrial estate and a map with a building circled. Important information indeed!

Picture Puzzle

Which building on the photograph is the one circled on the map?

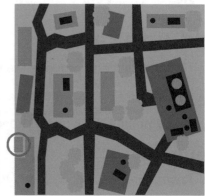

Action

What's My Job?

Rearrange the letters in the grid to spell out this job title. Use the light blue square letter twice.

Y	L	D
G		O
R	I	P

I'm a member of the film crew. I hold onto and push the trolley holding the camera, the camera operator and sometimes even the director!

____ ____ ____ ____ ____   ____ ____ ____

What's Missing?

Will you need a gold finger to finger the missing letter? Maybe the letter is for your eyes only, but even if the world is not enough, remember that even if you can't find it, tomorrow never dies…

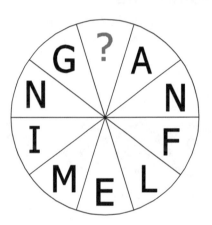

STORYBOARD 5

Ray-Son, the Mint Spy boss and electronics genius, breaks into the enemy's penthouse to plant a bug.

Picture Puzzle

Uh-oh! The *Dummies' Guide to Planting Bugs* has the instructions in the wrong order! Help Ray-Son out by numbering the instructions in the correct order.

○ Activate your personal warning system.

○ Be sure to first check the room is empty.

○ Extract the lamp's base and insert the bug.

○ Replace the base back onto the lamp.

○ Take out the lamp's plug from the power socket.

○ Then select a lamp in a suitable location.

○ You should finally check the bug is activated.

Code Red (or Blue?)

Brandy is the Mint Spies' codes expert. Test yourself against her expertise by solving these unusual codes. If you get stuck, Brandy has some tips on page 114 to get you started again.

Tea 4 Two

The enemy operatives finished their tea party and left these six cups behind. Aside from the different colours, it's interesting to note the unusual number of teaspoons in each cup. Decode the message to discover where the enemy plans to strike next.

Speeding Fine

Ray-Son has the pedal to the metal down this stretch of road but even he's confused by the speed signs. The signs are actually a code and they contain a cheery farewell.

STORYBOARD 6

It's another stake-out, but this time it's in an ice-cream van complete with an ultra-miniaturised communications dish.

Picture Puzzle

Look at the price list for the delectable products the Mint Spy's Ice Cream van sells. Use logic (and any clues you can find) to fill in the missing prices.

PRICE LIST

ice-cream:	$2.00
iced-cream:	$2.50
rice-cream:	$3.00
diced-cream:	$____
cider-cream:	$____
crier-cream:	$____

Calendar Code

The enemy operatives plan to strike on a very important Australian public holiday. But the only clues are these old calendars. Decode them to find the name of this annual event. The **1st** letter is from MAY **1st**. Which letter? The year is 2001 and it's **M**. The second letter is from DEC 2nd. Which letter? The year is 2002 and it's **E**. Extra points given if you can say which calendar page is actually the correct date for this event in the year given.

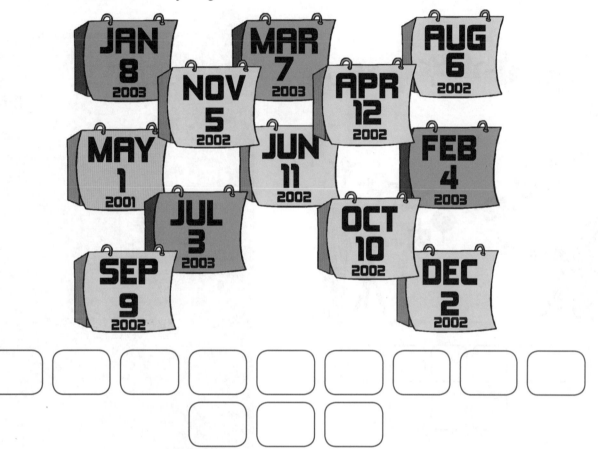

JAN 8 2003
MAR 7 2003
AUG 6 2002
NOV 5 2002
APR 12 2002
MAY 1 2001
JUN 11 2002
FEB 4 2003
JUL 3 2003
OCT 10 2002
SEP 9 2002
DEC 2 2002

I	N	G	E	W	A	R	N
O	P	E	R	N	E	M	Y
E	S	H	A	A	T	I	V
S	C	O	V	V	E	D	I
T	H	E	K	E	R	E	D
D	D	E	N	E	Y	H	I
R	B	A	C	U	N	D	E
R	M	A	T	K	D	O	O

Read 'em and Weep

The Mint Spies have intercepted this coded message. It's extremely important that they analyse, break and respond to the code. If the team had a pair of scissors they could solve it in a second. They don't, so it's up to you.

Action Film Trivia

The characters Gregorio, Carmen and Juni in the first *Spy Kids* movie are named after members of the director's family.

Action

Transmitter Trouble

The lab technicians are checking out their new toy; a laser-guided spy phone. It's working well, encoding the message before transmitting it across the open void of the lab. But the decoding is another matter ... If you'd like to eavesdrop on their conversation, just decide which of the numbers and letters are part of the message and which are meaningless rubbish. Then write the message symbols in the boxes provided.

Brandy's Clues

TEA 4 TWO

How many spoons in the red cup? What's the second letter of 'red'?

SPEEDING FINE

Which is the second letter of the alphabet?

CALENDAR CODE

12 pages... 12 dates... 3 years... 3-letter abbreviations...

READ 'EM AND WEEP

Scissors isn't enough for you? Do you really need to be told to cut it in half?

TRANSMITTER TROUBLE

How many sides does each shape have? Do the number of prongs match?

STORYBOARD 7

Ray-Son snaps a brilliant picture of an enemy operative sneaking into the building. What a pain it's blurred by the window!

Picture Puzzle

Which of the four silhouettes matches the person in the picture?

114

Action

Hollywood Crossquiz

It's up to the 'LLs' to light up Hollywood again. You know the drill; read the clue, fill in the missing letters and Bob Hollywood's your uncle!

clue								
side of a hill	**H**		**L**	**L**				
unusual, in a harmless way	**O**					**L**	**L**	
boiled lolly on a stick	**L**		**L**	**L**				
allowable by the law	**L**					**L**	**L**	
colour	**Y**		**L**	**L**				
tree with long, drooping branches	**W**		**L**	**L**				
more than full	**O**						**L**	**L**
authorised	**O**						**L**	**L**
child's toy	**D**		**L**	**L**				

STORYBOARD 8

An enemy operative sneaks out of the library, unaware of the Mint Spy on top of the bookshelf, poised to strike.

Picture Puzzle

The four bookshelves are all slightly different. Find the feature of each one that's different to the other three.

1. _____   2. _____

3. _____   4. _____

115

Cane Twisting

Ray-Son has a nifty cane that can twist into different shapes. With one lot of rearrangements of the cane what is the maximum number of triangles that can be formed? Ray's made the first one for you.

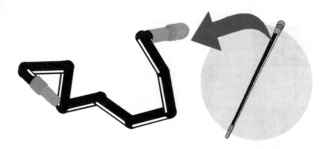

Action Film Trivia

The 'Austin Powers' films are spy movie spoofs. The first movie uses music, characters and dialogue from several James Bond films. The second and third films' titles are based on James Bond films: *The Spy Who Loved Me* and *Goldfinger*.

Spot the Difference

Look! Ray-Son's got some enemy spies in his sights.*

Actually he's got a whole bunch of spy words in his sights.

Actually he's got two groups of connected words in his sights.

Actually, there's one word in each of his sights that belongs in the other sight. But which ones? You may need to use a dictionary on a couple of the words!

* Actually they're not his sights at all.
  He pinched them off Brandy's desk. Hah!

STORYBOARD 9

The fight's on as Ray-Son is attacked by the knife-wielding, karate-kicking enemy operative.

Picture Puzzle

Ray-Son certainly has an extensive vocabulary of cartoon noises.
Funnily enough, all but one of these sounds has something in common. Which then, is the odd-sound-out?

Action

I Spy

It might not be a family tree but there's certainly a family of spies in it at the moment. I Spy with your little eye:

1. Two spies with identical hats and hat-bands
2. A pair of binoculars
3. A secret map
4. A telescope
5. How many spies altogether?

STORYBOARD 10

Cinna-Mon picks the lock on the safe door and takes off with the folder of top secret plans and flees the enemy HQ in her personal transporter.

Picture Puzzle

Remove one letter of TOP SECRET then rearrange the letters to answer the first clue. Write the removed letter in the coloured square. Repeat for each of the following clues. When you finish, rearrange all the letters in the coloured squares to identify Cinna-Mon's flying vehicle.

	T	O	P	S	E	C	R	E	T

upper branches and leaves of trees

rose like medal awarded as a prize

a road lined with buildings

to guide a vehicle

starting places for golf games

group of items

rotor powered flying vehicle (abbreviation)

117

Action

Information Update

The Mint Spies' secretary (Ms Moneycent) is updating the classified records. They're a bit of a muddle, so she'd certainly appreciate a hand. Read the information, then complete the chart with each spy's preferred martial art, favourite electronic device and arch enemy.

1. The villain XXL has poor eyesight and is usually captured in the dark by the spy with the night-vision goggles who doesn't know karate.
2. Ray-Son has scratches on his hands from trying to get his favourite spy-pen back from his pet Siamese cat.
3. Nut-Meg begins her 'empty hand' training sessions with a brief meditation.
4. The Count was defeated when his secret plans were folded into a paper crane by the spy who likes micro-waved food.
5. When Brandy defeated XXL she came home and washed her white cotton Judogi.
6. Nut-Meg borrowed Cinna-Mon's TV remote after she broke hers lobbing it at a fleeing Dr. Yes.

	Dr Yes	Count Von Badenuff	XXL	Pussikins	Spy-pen	Night vision goggles	TV remote	Microwave	Judo	Karate	Origami	Tae kwon do
Nut-Meg												
Brandy												
Cinna-Mon												
Ray-Son												
Judo												
Karate												
Origami												
Tae kwon do												
Spy-pen												
Night vision goggles												
TV remote												
Microwave												

	NUT-MEG	BRANDY	CINNA-MON	RAY-SON
Preferred Martial Art				
Favourite Electronic Device				
Arch Enemy				

118

Action

The Mint Spies: Afterburn® Trivia Quiz

Yes, it's the traditional end-of-the-chapter multiple-choice quiz. Remember, if you're going to cheat do it now before you start the quiz. Because then it's not really cheating is it? Oh, and just for fun (the author's, not yours), each question has a P in it.

1. In what PLACE does Brandy overhear the spies talking?
(a) A pizza shop
(b) A hamburger joint
(c) A car park
(d) A small pond

2. How many junior spies are in the PARK?
(a) none — it's a trick question
(b) just one — the question should read spy, not spies
(c) two — but one's hiding
(d) three — I just checked by looking

3. What does Nut-Meg take a PICTURE of?
(a) Her favourite goldfish, Goldfishfinger
(b) Her dumb sidekick, 3Ds (and no As …)
(c) A map; what else do spies take pictures of?
(d) Her finger on the lens cap

4. What two tall, cylindrical objects are on the roof of the building in the PHOTOGRAPH?
(a) An un-detectable spy (so prove me wrong!)
(b) Two chimneys who are much too young to smoke
(c) A cat litter tray (and cat)
(d) A roof-lovers' convention

5. Where does Ray-Son PLANT the listening bug?
(a) In his garden; it's where they grow best
(b) In the lamp, because someone else had planted a bulb there
(c) In the fridge; he thought it was an ear of corn
(d) Ear and there

6. What type of PRODUCE was the spy-van selling?
(a) Spice
(b) Ice cream
(c) Spyders
(d) Spy-nach

7. What did Ray-Son see through the PANE of glass?
(a) A spy? (Well, duh!)
(b) A pane-ter?
(c) A pane-t-brush?
(d) A pane-o-ramic view?

8. What was in the PITCH-black room?
(a) Er, darkness?
(b) A good title for a Science Fiction film
(c) A spy with perfect pitch
(d) Bookshelves

9. Which of these words didn't Ray-Son exclaim when he was PUNCHED?
(a) Ouch!
(b) Eek!
(c) Uuh!
(d) !$**@#!

10. What two words were written on the PORTFOLIO?
(a) TOP SECRET
(b) FOR YOUR EYES ONLY
(c) PLEASE OPEN
(d) TWO WORDS

Learning More

PLACES

Taj Mahal
www.taj-mahal.net

Statue of Liberty
www.nps.gov/stli

Pyramids
www.memphis.edu/egypt/giza.htm

Sydney Opera House
www.sydneyoperahouse.com

ACTIVITIES

Fingerprint Cards
www.fbi.gov/kids/k5th/whatwedo2.htm

FILMS

Spy Kids
www.spykids.com

James Bond
www.ianfleming.org/index.shtml

INTERNATIONAL SPY MUSEUM

www.spymuseum.org/index.asp

Creative Holiday Learning Year 6

Answers

ANSWERS

WELCOME

Page xiv

Out and About the Lot
This is the path they took on their tour:

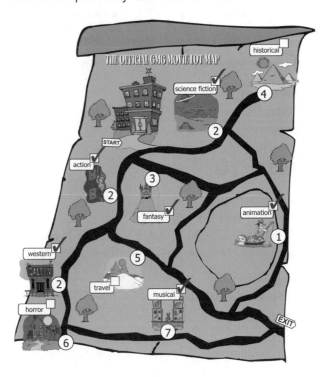

In order, the sets were SCience Fiction, Animation, FaNtasy, ACtion, WEstern and MusicaL. The studio intends to CANCEL the others.

SCIENCE FICTION

Page 2

Starbeamers III
Starbeamers VIIII is misspelt; it should be VIII (8).

Gross Science Fiction Films
(Jurassic) Park 1993, (Independence) Day 1996, (Phantom) Menace 1999, (Attack of the) Clones 2002, (Men in) Black 1997, (Star) Wars 1977, (Return of the) Jedi 1983, (Fifth) Element 1998, (Planet of the) Apes 2001, (Back to the) Future 1985

Page 3

Anagrammaticals
1. SPACE SHIP, 2. UNIVERSE, 3. BLACK HOLE , 4. OUTER SPACE

Quick Numbers
1. III, 2. three, 3. three alien fingers

Page 4

Synopsis Search
HEY WHAT'S SATURN DOING ON YOUR HEAD?

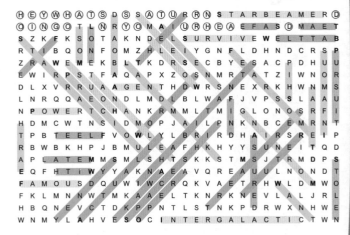

Page 5

3D Navigation

  6

2

 5

 1

  3

  4

ANSWERS

Storyboard 1

The numbers represent the days in the months starting from January (mentioned in the story). The next number in sequence will be 31 (days in August).

Page 6

Jumbled Director
GEORGE LUCAS

Storyboard 2
Tricky: a five-letter palindromic word. Clue? The diamond shape is red and so is the letter A formed on the dashboard. The story mentions 'anti-detection screens' — could the word be RADAR? (Um, yes!)

Page 7

Hollywood Crossquiz
handbill, originally, locally, lullaby, yell, wallet, overalls, outsell, dolly

Storyboard 3
TENT — SENT — PENS — PINS — SHIP

Page 8

Movie Matrix

M	E		T	S
D	O	L	L	Y
C	A	V	E	S
T	H	E	I	R
T	A	S	T	E

Make-up Magic
Di Gussie is what we call an unknown star. And talking of stars, did you notice each of the actors had a star on them? Except for D. (That's Deb—Di's double.)

Storyboard 4
Any of the dimensions could give you a volume of 240 m³, but trailer (a) would be just 5 m long and (c) would be 8 m long. Best bet is (b) at a length of 20 m.

Page 9

Movie Match-up
The film was ALIEN.

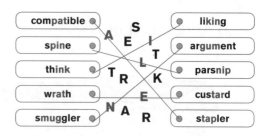

Storyboard 5
25 flags. 25 x 100,000 = 2,500,000 rivets! C'est magnifique!

Page 10

Planet Shuffle
Start: J-S-U-N-E-V-Ma-Me-P
1. Me-J-S-U-N-E-V-Ma-P   3. Me-V-E-J-S-U-N-Ma-P
2. Me-V-J-S-U-N-E-Ma-P   4. Me-V-E-Ma-J-S-U-N-P

Planet Words
1. menu, 2. mumps, 3. Venus (!) 4. sun

Storyboard 6
Base (smallest) 20 m Pedestal 27 m
Statue (largest) 46 m

Page 11

ARFS
ACE – hero – 1 film – $100,000
PASH – scientist – three films – $2,500,000
VINE – camper – two films – $300,000

Here's how you could have worked it out:

1. The hero makes the least money. We can tick the HERO-$100,000 square. A cross goes in the other options (of the hero earning other amounts or the other roles earning $100,000) as these are false.

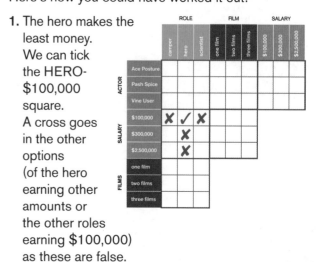

122

ANSWERS

2. Pash has been in the most films. Tick the PASH-THREE FILMS square. Add a cross to the other options as they are now false.

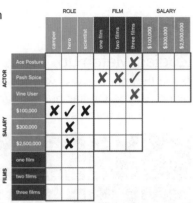

3. Ace would like to play a scientist one day. Now we know that Ace wasn't the scientist.

4. The camper makes more money than Ace but less than Pash. This is a biggy! This tells us that neither Ace nor Pash are the camper. So tick the VINE-CAMPER square and cross the others. It also gives us the money amounts: Ace then the Camper (Vine) then Pash. So we can complete the SALARY/ ACTOR section. Since Vine is the camper and Ace isn't the scientist Pash must be the scientist. That leaves Ace as the hero. We also now know that the scientist (Pash) has made three films.

5. The actor on $300,000 negotiated a pay rise for the second film. This finishes things off nicely: the $300,000 actor is Vine. If it's the second film they made more than one film. But they didn't make three (because Pash did). So Vine made two.

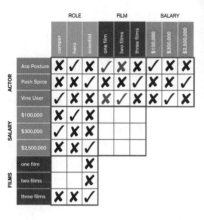

Storyboard 7
There are three pairs of west/east movements so the aliens finish where they started in those directions. But there are three norths and only two souths so they must end up NORTH.

Page 12

Spiral Galaxy
Spaceship 1
a. six **b.** atlas **c.** rats **d.** never **e.** eel **f.** ping **g.** rob **h.** lion **i.** row

Spaceship 2
a. worn **b.** oil **c.** Borg **d.** nip **e.** leer **f.** even **g.** star **h.** salt **i.** axis

Storyboard 8
21 tiles are missing

Page 13

What's My Job?
BOOM OPERATOR

Spot the Silhouette
Silhouette E is the matching spacecraft.

Storyboard 9
J: the letters are the initials of the planets in our solar system.

ANSWERS

Page 14

The Final Countdown
The numbers are in reverse alphabetical order. Missing (in action) are FOUR, FIVE and EIGHT.

What's Next
The missing letter is the E at the end of JULES VERNE, author of *Journey to the Centre of the Earth*, *From the Earth to the Moon* and *20,000 Leagues Under the Sea*.

Storyboard 10
1. The small red spaceship has moved.
2. The pig has gained an extra eye.
3. And lost its red snout.
4. And gained a smile (it likes the new eye).
5. And has an extra turn in its tail.
6. The star above the spaceship turned nova (and became bigger).
7. The alien's eye is now looking up. (surprised at the pig's new eye no doubt).
8. And its clipboard-recorder thingy has changed colour.
9. And it's gained a new pocket too.
10. One crater has disappeared.

Page 15

From S to F
SCARF, SMURF, STUFF, SERIF, SNUFF, SNIFF, SCOFF, STIFF, STAFF, SHELF.

The red letters spell out 'ARTIFICIAL' (AI is an abbreviation for Artificial Intelligence.)

Page 16

Southern Constellations
PICTOR – Painter's Easel

CHAMAELEON – Chameleon

CENTAURUS – Centaur

HYDRUS – Water Snake

TUCANA – Toucan

TRIANGULUM AUSTRALE – Triangle

CRUX – Southern Cross

ARA – Altar

Page 17

Zodiac Match-up
If you thought this was way too hard you're not alone. Maybe the ancient stargazers had better imaginations than us?

Page 19

Trivia Quiz
1. (c) dodgem cars
2. (b) red. Yes, it's transparent in some pictures but red in storyboard 2.
3. (c) mountains
4. (a) zero
5. (d) the ground
6. (a) the Statue of Liberty
7. (d) hamburgers
8. (d) Australia
9. (b) huge spot
10. (a) pig (with three eyes)

Page 20

What's the Shot?
MS - CU - WS - EWS - ECU- MCU

Popular tourist attraction: MUSEUM

Page 21

Shoot for the Moon
Left

reflection, split screen, sub-clip, tilted horizon

Right

object POV, mask vignette, silhouette, dramatic angle

ANSWERS

ANIMATION

Page 22

Hardly Original

Unscramble the letters making up each of the four figures and you have:

1. REPLICA 2. ORIGINAL 3. FORGERY and
4. COUNTERFEIT

Hardly Rhyming
BLACKSMITH

Page 23

Poster Posers
Anagrammaticals
1. DOCTOR 2. SCHOOL TEACHER 3. DENTIST
4. HAIRDRESSER 5. LUMBERJACK

Quick Count
12 words begin with HAR.

Page 24

Blank Cheques

Cheque I is on top.

Cheque A is at the bottom.

Cheque F has Cathie Jones's name spelt Cathie Janes.

Cheques B and H have identical numbers (2991).

Cheque No 2990 is missing.

There are four different whole numbers less than 12,345 with 5s in them: 5555, 555, 55 and 5. The sum of these is 6170. If we could use each number twice then the sum would be 12,340. Add the $3 cheque we already have and the sum is now 12,343 — just $2 shy of our mark. But the question asked for eight different cheques. Add 50c to one of each duplicate and we end up with nine cheques: $5555.00, $5555.50, $555.00, $555.50, $55.00, $55.50, $5.00, $5.50 and the existing $3.00 which is totally exactly $12,345.00.

Page 25

Synopsis Search
Harriet, I've had bitter jobs than this one.

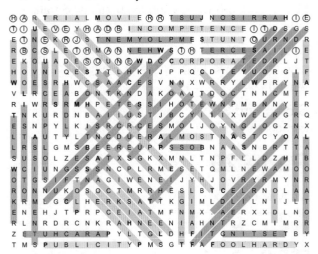

Page 26

Jumbled Director
WALT DISNEY

Storyboard 1
Hardly is wearing Tie 4.

Page 27

D-Day
a. DECORATOR b. DRIVER
c. DOCTOR d. DEALER
e. DANCER f. DRAPER
g. DOWSER h. DEBATER
i. DRUMMER j. DENTIST
k. DROVER l. DIETITIAN

```
D E C O R A T O R
D D D D D D D D D
R O E A R O E R E
I C A N A W B U N
V T L C P S A M T
E O E E E E T M I
R R R R R R E E S
D R O V E R R R T
D I E T I T I A N
```

Storyboard 2
Tricky…

Okay, now BRIEF CASE is in capitals, so it must be important. Funnily enough it has the same number of letters as all the things inside it. A careful look at the case reveals the letters CCVVC CVCV which just so happens to be the template for the Consonants and Vowels in BRIEF CASE. So that's why CREAM CAKE (CCVVC CVCV) is in but LEMON CAKE (CVCVC CVCV) isn't. That also means that Hardly has a GREEN BIRO in his case.

ANSWERS

Page 28

Desk Mess
Envelope Clues
birth, guard, drown, eve, loo, crab, gums, Sarah, tape, tag

Telephone Clues
gate, pat, harass, mug, bar, cool, even, word, draught, rib

Storyboard 3
Parachute 1

Page 29

Movie Matrix

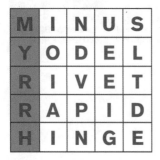

M	I	N	U	S
Y	O	D	E	L
R	I	V	E	T
R	A	P	I	D
H	I	N	G	E

Pyramid Power
Start in the light coloured stone. 10 + ? = 17, so that stone must be **7**. The 7 stone is the sum of the two stones below (? + 4) so we now have the centre stone in the bottom row: **3**. ? + 3 = 10, so the second stone in the bottom row is also **7**. The rest of the stones should be quite easy to calculate now.

70
36 34
19 17 17
9 10 7 10
2 7 3 4 6

Storyboard 4

POLITEST
SPOTLIT
PISTOL
PILOT
SPOILT
TOPSOIL
COPILOTS

Page 30

Free Advice

I	T	'	S		A		J	O	B		N	E	V	E	R
S	T	A	R	T	E	D		T	H	A	T		T	A	K	E	S
T	H	E		L	O	N	G	E	S	T		T	O		F	I	N	I	S	H

Hardly MD
Negative 3

Storyboard 5
Day one's fish added up to 38. Since the Snuppies are worth 13, the most he could have tagged are two — a total of 26 — leaving 12 points to share between an Angelic fish and a Freon.

Day two's fish added up to 36 points — 2 points less than day 1. They must have been two Snuppies and two Angelics.

Day three is a good day (40 points). Two Snuppies and two Freons.

Page 31

How Was Work Today?
Wow! Fifteen bad puns in one puzzle! Here we go:

'So Hardly, how was work today …

a. …as a bricklayer?
'I've cemented some good friendships.' (9)

b. …as a merry-go-round tester?
'I don't know; my head's still in a spin.' (4)

c. …as a meteorologist?
'I don't know weather I'll be there long.' (8)

d. …as a swimming instructor?
'I'm in way above my head.' (5)

e. …as a window washer?
'A real pane.' (6)

f. …as an opera singer?
'I hit a few high notes.' (11)

g. …at the chimney factory?
'It doesn't stack up to my other jobs.' (10)

h. …at the clock shop?
'The boss really ticked me off.' (14)

i. …at the marmalade factory?
'I jammed my foot in a machine.' (15)

j. …at the opticians?
'I don't think I'll see it through.' (3)

k. …down on the farm?
'It's one crop of problems after another.' (13)

ANSWERS

l. …in the banana shop?
'Terrible—I kept slipping up.' (2)

m. …in the book shop?
'Busy; my pager went non-stop.' (12)

n. …in the sewing shop?
'Fred the boss is always needling me.' (1)

o. …taxi driving?
'Fare.' (7)

Storyboard 6

Hardly starts submerged completely. Every two minutes he pushes himself out 20 cm then sinks back 15 cm. His progress then is 5 cm every two minutes, or 2.5 cm/minute. So does he need 72 minutes (180/2.5) to extract himself? No, because after just 64 minutes he's pulled himself out 160 cm. In the following minute he pulls himself out the next 20 cm and is completely free. So it takes just 65 minutes. Of course, Hardly left his hat behind and had to go back for it, adding another 3 hours to the task. But that's another puzzle…

Page 32

Cartoon Characters

Yabba Dabba Do Da!	FRED FLINTSTONE
To infinity and beyond!	BUZZ LIGHTYEAR
D'oh	HOMER SIMPSON
Minnie Mouse	MICKEY MOUSE
Beep Beep!	ROAD RUNNER
What's up doc?	BUGS BUNNY
Odie	GARFIELD
I tawt I taw a puddy tat!	TWEETIE
Charlie Brown	SNOOPY
Roar!	SIMBA
Don't have a cow!	BART
Stimpy	REN

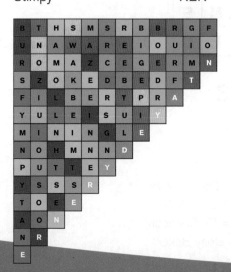

Page 33

What's My Job
ANIMATORS

ROW + DS = WORDS
1. ARROW 2. BROWN 3. CROWD 4. WORRY
5. WORMS 6. SWORD 7. GROWL 8. FROWN
9. WORLD 10. SWORE

Storyboard 7
Yellow has an extra N.

Storyboard 8
Seven arrows remain. That's how many hit Hardly.

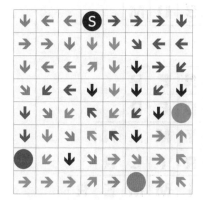

Page 34

Hollywood Crossquiz
hoodlum, onlooker, loop, loosen, Yankee Doodle, woolly, ooze, overshoot, drool

Brick Out
Cube 1 has 23 bricks, cube 2 has 21 bricks and cube 3 has 21 bricks.

Storyboard 9
Net 4 can't be folded into a brick.

Page 35

Hardly Heaven
It really couldn't be anything else than that classic song 'Stairway To Heaven'. You get an extra bonus point if you knew the name of the band! (Led Zeppelin).

Storyboard 10
All the chords use four fingers (one for each dot) and a couple are a bit tricky for new guitarists to get their hands around. But actually wrong? Hmm, that **first chord** has two circles on one string, which would be a little pointless…

ANSWERS

Page 36

Unusual Occupations
A SCHRIMP SCHONGER

S	A	W	Y	E	R				
C	A	P	E	R					
H	E	L	L	O		G	I	R	L
R	A	T	O	N	E	R			
I	C	E	M	A	N				
M	O	N	D	A	Y		M	A	N
P	L	U	M	B	U	M			

S	P	O	O	N	E	R			
C	H	O	W	D	E	R			
H	A	N	K	Y	M	A	N		
O	U	T	C	R	I	E	R		
N	I	M	G	I	M	M	E	R	
G	L	I	M	M	E	R		M	A	N
E	Y	E	R						
R	O	P	E	R					

Page 38

Hardly Working

Dancer: weekend — paper cut — $150
Decorator: one day — false teeth — $0.15
Dentist: one week — twisted ankle — $1.50
Dramatist: one day — wallpaper glue — $15.00

Page 39

Trivia Quiz
Every answer is C!

Page 40

Script to Sound Track
1. asynchronous sound effects 2. narration
3. synchronous sound effects 4. dialogue
5. local music 6. dialogue 7. synchronous sound
effects 8. synchronous sound effects 9. dialogue
10. background music

Page 41

Instrument Squares
Saxophone, c**Y**mbal, violi**N**, **T**rumpet, was**H**board,
flut**E**, bas**S**oon, p**I**ano, drum**S**, trombon**E**, guita**R**.
The missing instrument is a SYNTHESISER.

MUSIC

Page 42

Back to Front (the musical)
MAB CROAK. All the others are anagrams of
BACKROOM.

Magic-band Magic-square

M	U	S	I	C
U	L	U	R	U
S	U	P	E	R
I	R	E	N	E
C	U	R	E	D

Page 43

Poster Posers
Anagrammaticals

1. lead guitar = Gu Araldite
2. lead vocals = Dallas Cove
3. bass guitar = Guab Sitars
4. percussion = Pu Ericsson
5. keyboards = Dosy Baker

ANSWERS

Capital Sentence

Each capital begins with the last letter of the city before it. So either Moscow or Manila would fit. Out of the two, Manila is better; it ends in A which is the first letter of the first city (Athens).

Page 44

Synopsis Search

What is a drummer?

A PERSON WHO HANGS OUT WITH MUSICIANS.

Which is a little rude, especially if you are a drummer. To even things out, what is a musician? A drummer's roadie. That's funnier if you've ever been a drummer in a band…

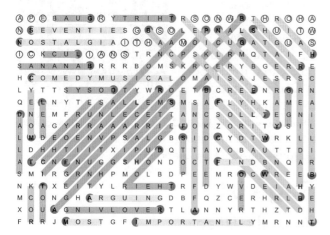

Page 45

Turn It Up

A: 52

Why? Increasing time units. There are 60 seconds in a minute, 60 minutes in an hour, 24 hours in a day, 7 days in a week and 52 weeks in a year. We'll also accept 2 (weeks in a fortnight).

B: 13

Why? Prime numbers from 3.

C: 31

Why? Days in the months of the year. January has 31, February has 28 (often!), March has 31, April has 30 and then May has 31.

D: 26

The next number is 2 larger than the gap between the two previous numbers. 5−2=3, 10−5=5 (2 larger than 3), 17−10=7 (2 larger than 5). The next gap must be 2 larger than 7. 17+2+7=26.

Movie Matrix

M	I	X	E	R
Y	O	U	N	G
N	O	V	E	L
A	U	D	I	O
H	E	D	G	E

Storyboard 1

No, you can't draw it in one continuous line (without cheating!).

Page 46

Hollywood Crossquiz

HIGHWAY, OWLISH, LIGHTWEIGHT, LOW PITCHED, YELLOWISH, WHITEWASH, OVERTHROW, OVERWEIGHT, DISHWASHER

Storyboard 2

1. thunderstorm **2.** light rain **3.** fog **4.** smoke/smog **5.** lightning **6.** tornado **7.** moderate snow **8.** thunderstorm and rain

Page 47

Jumbled Director

Randal Kleiser

Storyboard 3

Toilet 2; it has a green indicator.

Page 48

Damp-Amp

A – 4, B – 3, C – 5, D – 2, E – 1
D is about to get fried.

Storyboard 4

Page 49

What's My Job

SOUND ENGINEER

ANSWERS

Cold As Christmas

1. Jingle Bells
2. Frosty the Snowman
3. The Twelve Days of Christmas
4. Silent Night
5. We Wish You A Merry Christmas

Storyboard 5

He is, of course, saying what all sound guys say:

T	E	S	T	I	N	G
T	E	S	T	I	N	G
O	N	E	■	T	W	O
T	H	R	E	E	■	■

Page 50

Fussy Eaters

The food preferences can only contain vowels that are in the band member's surname. So Pu Ericsson wants the swordfish, Gu Araldite wants the red mandarins (do you know how hard THEY are to find?), Dallas Cove wants the chowder, Dosy Baker wants the waffles and Guab Sitars wants the rabbit (preferably white, for her party trick).

Storyboard 6

Start with the last information given. A2+A3=A5. Since 1 is already taken we can only use the numbers 2,3,4 and 5. A5 must equal 5 as this is the only number that is the sum of two other numbers.

We don't know yet which of A2 and A3 equal 2 or 3, but we do know that A4 must equal 4 — it's the only number left in that row. Similarly, B4 must also equal 5 and B1 is 4.

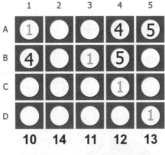

Now we can fill in D4—it must be 2, to make the column add up to 12. Look at column 5. The 5 and 1 add up to 6. The missing two numbers must total 7, to make the column total of 13.

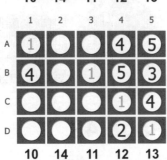

The missing numbers could be 5+2 or 4+3. Since we already have a 5 in that column, they must be 4 and 3. Row B has a 4 in it already, so it must go in C5 and the 3 in B5.

Next, complete row B with a 2 in B2. Because no columns can contain the same numbers A2 (which was either 2 or 3) must be 3, and A3 must be 2.

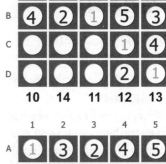

C1 + D1 must equal 5. A1 and B1 already contain 1 and 4 so the empty spaces must contain 3 and 2. Row D already has a 2 in it, so D1 must be 3 and C1 must be 2. Column 2 adds up to 14, so C2 + D2 equal 9. C2 must be 5 (there's already a 4 in row C) and D2 must be 4. Row C has a 3 missing from it and row D a 5. The number 5 buttons are A5, B4, C2 and D3.

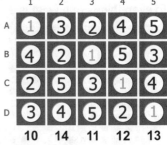

Page 51

Ralph the Roadie

Wind Me Up

Lead 3 is the only lead coiled clockwise. And Ralph the Roadie is many things, but being wise about clocks isn't one of them.

Last Lead

The red one. All the other leads have another lead on top of them.

Storyboard 7

When this song becomes a hit, remember you saw it here first. Hope that ABBA doesn't sue on the last line.

H	E	Y	■	B	A	B	Y	■	I
L	O	V	E	■	Y	O	U	,	■
H	E	Y	■	B	A	B	Y	■	■
I	T	'	S	■	T	R	U	E	.
H	E	Y	■	B	A	B	Y	■	I
L	O	V	E	■	Y	O	U	,	■
Y	E	S	■	I	■	D	O	,	■
I	■	D	O	,	I	■	D	O	!

130

ANSWERS

Page 52

Take Your Pick

Storyboard 8
Skedaddled.

This is a set-up of course, but how? For starters, the number you pick makes no difference as multiplying by nine and adding the digits together will always give nine. Adding one to your answer makes ten and so we've forced the letter J upon you. Hmm, countries beginning with J? Japan, Jamaica and Jordan. Guess what, the last vowel in each country is an A! Counting forward 3 gives you D and so the answer is Skedaddled.

Page 53

Band Names

Row 1 – strip D, row 2 – strip A, row 3 – strip E, row 4 – strip B, row 5 – strip F, row 6 – strip H, row 7 – strip G, row 8 – strip C.

B	R	B	A	R	C	M	K
R	O	B	O	R	O	K	C
O	B	O	O	O	O	A	M
C	C	O	C	A	M	B	R
O	C	A	O	C	R	K	A
C	R	R	O	K	O	A	B
M	R	O	M	A	K	R	M
R	K	O	A	O	K	K	M

Storyboard 9
JANET, ALEXA, BRUNO and SIMON

Page 54

Rock Around the Clock

1. BLACK **2.** WHISK **3.** SLEEK **4.** PLANK
5. SHOCK **6.** SHARK **7.** FLASK **8.** CREEK
9. KAYAK

The band leader was Bill Haley.

Blow Your Stack

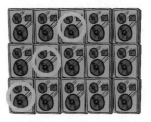

Storyboard 10
The plastic cup next to his foot. It doesn't show a spike hole.

Page 55

Hit or Miss

Side A
(a) DROWN (b) ROW (c) SEE (d) BAT (e) LET
(f) OHP (g) SAW (h) DIRT (i) SALAD (j) NAP

Side B
(a) PANDA (b) LAST (c) RID (d) WASP (e) HOTEL
(f) TA (g) BEES (h) WORN (i) WORD

Page 56

Rock Trivia Quiz

Start question: answer is guitar (red)	Letter = S
S question: answer 1950s (red)	Letter = H
H question: answer is disk jockey (blue)	Letter = A
A question: answer is Rock Around… (blue)	Letter = M
M question: answer is lead guitar (blue)	Letter = R
R question: answer is Sun Records (blue)	Letter = O
O question: answer is bass (red)	Letter = C
C question: answer is Motor Town (blue)	Letter = K
K question: answer is California (blue)	CD 2
Head off to D (via black arrow)	Letter = D
D question: answer is 1964 (red)	Letter = U
U question: answer is Jamaica (red)	Letter = B
B question: answer is folk rock (blue)	Letter = L
L question: answer is guitar solos (red)	Letter = I
I question: answer is The UK (blue)	Letter = N
N question: answer is disco (blue)	CD 1

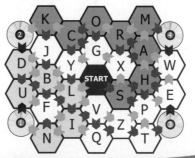

Band SHAMROCK, city DUBLIN, CDs 2 and 1

ANSWERS

Page 57

Music to Go
THE BANGUI TARENTELLA
RAZOR SHARP
CYBORG ANTHEM
SWINE FLU TEQUILA
RED RUM RUMBLE

DRUM	F A N C Y T H A T
FLUTE	I D L E D R I F T
GUITAR	T V M A N A W A Y
HARP	V A G U E L O I S
ORGAN	A N T S D I A R Y

A D V A N C E   A U S T R A L I A   F A I R

Like Peas in a Pod
a. The song is labelled 02, not 01
b. Red button
c. Black button
d. Extra black stripe
e. Extra button above screen

Page 58

Back to Front
Some hints before the answers:

Clue 1 gives us Gu's annoying habit and band.
Clue 2 helps a little. Gu isn't the garlic eater so she can't be the highest singer.
Clue 3 provides all the information about Dallas.
Clue 4 mentions 'Smelly' which is Gu's band.
Clue 5 tells us that Dosy isn't the snorer and wasn't in Funky.

DALLAS is always tapping, sings a C and was in Icky.
DOSY loves garlic, sings high G and was in Stinky.
GU talks in her sleep, sings a D and was in Smelly.
GUAB snores, sings up to an E and was in Funky.

Page 59

The Back to Front Trivia Quiz
All the answers are C.

FILM SCHOOL
stunts

Page 60

Stunt Puzzle 1
Stella has 4 planes, Stan has 2 planes. If Stella gave Stan a plane they'd both have three.
If Stan gave Stella a plane she'd have 5 and he'd have just 1.

Stunt Puzzle 2
1. Stevie **2.** Stone **3.** Steph **4.** Stacey **5.** Stu

Stunt Puzzle 3
It's in the van.

Stunt Puzzle 4
There are quite a few pairs of prime numbers that add up to 30 including 7 and 23, 11 and 19 and 13 and 17. But only the last pair has a difference of 4.

Stunt Puzzle 5
If Stella jumps 16 vehicles the distance would be only 48 m. So she jumps 17 cars for a distance of 51 m, beating the record by 1.4 m.

Stunt Puzzle 6
One way to solve this is to simply consider each person in turn. Was it Stuart?
Two statements say it was but only one statement can be true so it wasn't Stuart. Was it Stella?
Once again, two statements say it was, so they must be false. Was it Stan? Only one statement says it was and this must be the true statement.

Page 61

The World's Most Prolific Stuntman
VICTOR MONROE ARMSTRONG

ANSWERS

WESTERN

Page 62

Lightning Jock

Cross out 1 and 7 (Canadian states) 4, 5 and 9 (US states nowhere near the Wild West), 6 (India) and 8 and 10 (Australian). Leaving us with just 2 and 3.

Great Westerns

Stagecoach, Tombstone, Wyatt Earp, High Noon, True Grit, Blazing Saddles, Dodge City, Butch Cassidy

(The) GREAT TRAIN ROBBERY

Page 63

Poster Posers

Anagrammaticals
1. BAD GUY IN BLACK 2. RUDE SCOTSMAN
3. DUMB SHERIFF 4. BRAVE BRAVE
5. SASSY COWGIRL 6. OLD PROSPECTOR

Quick Numbers

There are 24 bullet holes on the poster.

Page 64

Synopsis Search

IT DEPENDS ON HOW HARD YOU CAN THROW

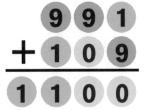

Page 65

Slanging Match

thrown by a horse	G	1	grassed
cigarette	R	6	seegar
gaol house	E	4	pokey
coward	E	2	yellow belly
carrying a weapon	N	6	packin'
ridiculous	H	1	horse feathers
crazy	O	2	loco
dead	R	6	buzzard food
talking nonsense	N	3	windbagging

Storyboard 1
70, 23 and 7

Page 66

Jumbled Director

John Ford

Storyboard 2
GOLD > CLOG > COGS > HOGS > GASH > CASH

Page 67

Hollywood Crossquiz

HARPOON, OUTDOOR, LOONY, LAMPOON, YAHOO, WASHROOM, OUTLOOK, ODDLOOKING, DOOR

Drinks are on the House

$$991 + 109 = 1100$$

Storyboard 3

1. 20 windows.

2. It's tempting to think 4 x 4 but the four corner posts are shared. So it's actually (4 x 2) + 4 = 12 verandah posts.

ANSWERS

Page 68

Card Sharp
1. Hand 4 is worth 44 points.

2. Hand 1 has just a pair. Hand 2 has three of a kind. Hand 4 has two pairs but Hand 3 has three of a kind *and* a pair – also known as a 'full house'.

3. The Queen of Diamonds is in Hands 1 and 4.

One More Card
1. The card value changes by 3 each time so the next value card has to be a 3 (skipping the Ace and 2). Which of the two threes? The suit sequence is clubs, diamonds, hearts then spades then clubs. The 3 of diamonds (card 2) is next.

2. A simple backwards sequence that skips 2 cards each time. The next card is the Queen of Hearts, card 2.

Storyboard 4
Each number stands for a letter of the alphabet. So far the letters spell out SHAK. An E (letter 5) would complete the drink name. The clues were the picture of the milkshake and the mention of the drink.

Page 69

Movie Matrix

M	O	U	S	E
N	O	R	T	H
N	A	V	A	L
A	G	A	I	N
S	N	O	R	E

Gunning for a Word
GUNK, BEGUN, BURGUNDY

Storyboard 5
Boots 2 and 5 are identical.

Page 70

In Gaol for a Spell

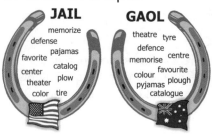

Storyboard 6
The code is ! 6 ? # – & ≠
J A I L S M W

The code words are:

JAIL ! 6 ? #

LISA # ? – 6

MAIL & 6 ? #

SALAMI – 6 # 6 & ?

SAW-MILL – 6 ≠ – & ? # #

Page 71

Tee-Hee a Teepee
PEEWEE, GEEGEE, SQUEEGEE, QUEEN-BEE, TWEEDLEDEE

Good Intent
Map 4 is the correct match.

Storyboard 7
Yes, it's tent 25. Because that's the only odd tent…

Page 72

Go West!

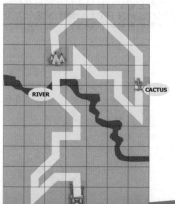

ANSWERS

Storyboard 8
The black trail adds up to 50. The red trail is 49 and the blue trail 51.

Page 73

What's my Job?
SCENIC ARTIST

Wagon Wheelies
1. N

Why? They're compass directions.

2. OE

Why? A little tricky this one. The letters are the initials of the degrees in a circle. Z is zero, FF is forty-five, N is ninety, OTF is one thirty five and the missing segment is OE – one eighty.

3. E

Why? Initial letters again, but this time of the whole numbers from One to Eight.

4. U

Why? The letters spell out the word 'CIRCULAR', starting anti-clockwise from the bottom C.

Storyboard 9
The only required measurement is that of the wagon wheels. The circumference of the wheel is roughly 3.14 times the wheel's diameter; about 5 m. One thousand revolutions gives a distance of about 5 km. Of course, Jock could have also just read the sign a few metres along the trail.

Page 74

Quick Count
There are 21 arrows in the hat. That cowboy's one sharp dresser!

Smoke Signals

Storyboard 10
Sequence three is the only one with the colours in alphabetical order: Green, Orange, Pink then Yellow.

Page 75

Desert Trek
Cowboy A
(a) MINE (b) DUNG (c) GUN (d) STAB (e) POOR
(f) DRAW (g) WOLF (h) SPA (i) TRIAL

Cowboy B
(a) LAIR (b) TAPS (c) FLOW (d) WAR (e) DROOP
(f) BAT (g) SNUG (h) GNU (i) DENIM

Page 76

Your Place or Mine?
1. LARIAT – A (lasso)
2. APPALOOSA – B (horse)
3. REVOLVER – A (gun)
4. MUSTANG – B (horse)
5. UNDERCUT – C (cut under an ore body)
6. CHAPS – D (over-trousers)
7. SHAFT – C (mine hole)
8. SALT LAKE – E (lake filled with salt water)
9. CANTEEN – A (water bottle)
10. ANVIL – F (metal block used for hammering on)
11. BUTTE – E (hill)
12. KERCHIEF – D (scarf)
13. PAINT – B (horse)
14. SKIP – C (container for putting useless ore in)
15. JEANS – D (trousers)
16. ORE – C (rock with metal in it)

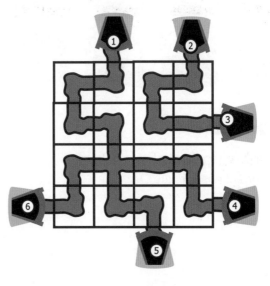

ANSWERS

Page 77

Horse Tales

Hints

Clue 1: Jock's horse isn't Goldie. Only one pair of horses are separated by just one hand in height.

Clue 4: Put the information in this clue with clue 1 together with the information that the other pair of horses are the shortest and tallest, and you'll know the names and heights of Jock and Clementine's horses.

Solution

LIGHTNING JOCK: Has a horse named Heather (naturally!) that eats toffees and is 13 hands high.

CLEMENTINE has a horse called Goldie (funny about that) who likes sugar cubes and is 14 hands high.

DAN GOOLIE has a horse called Cactus who eats lettuce sandwiches and is just 11 hands high.

THE SHERIFF has a horse called Sandy who likes bananas and is 18 hands high.

Page 78

Wanted: Better Wanted Posters

Cowboy number 5 isn't wanted. Except by his mummy.

Page 79

The Lightning Jock Trivia Quiz

All the correct answers are D.

Page 80

World Ratings

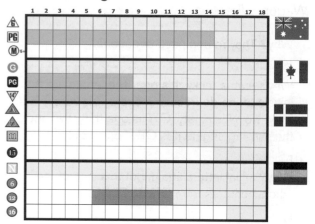

Page 81

What's My Classification?

Star Wars PG

Lord of the Rings: The Fellowship of the Ring M

Shrek PG

Spy Kids 3D PG

Harry Potter and the Philosopher's Stone G

Gone in 60 Seconds M

The Wizard of Oz G

The Princess Diaries G

Grease PG

Charlie's Angels (Full Throttle) M

ANSWERS

FANTASY

Page 82

Elf Guard: The Book

The dragon has turned PURPLE, the replica doesn't look much like the jester, Purtle's conch shell has changed into a hunting horn, Pixle doesn't appear to tower over anybody and the Teapot of Doom's unicorn is now a bird.

Black Mountain Castle

Castle 6 matches the silhouette.

Page 83

Poster Posers

Anagrammaticals

1. Lord of the Rings **2.** Harry Potter **3.** The Wizard of Oz **4.** Shrek **5.** Alice in Wonderland

Page 84

Synopsis Search

ELFY, WEALTHY AND WISE!

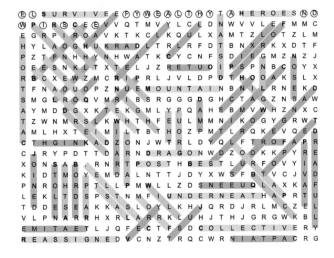

Page 85

Jumbled Director

PETER JACKSON

Page 86

Crossword Scramble

Storyboard 1

There are four spectres (circled) and the teapot is in the upstairs room.

Page 87

Magic Spells

FROG > FORT > FONT > NOTE > TOED > **TOAD**

GOLD > CLOG > COAL > **TACO**

TEAPOT > ROTATE > TARGET > GUTTER > TRUDGE > **GRUDGE**

QUEST > QUIET > EQUIP > TIEUP > TULIP > PILOT > **TOILS**

Storyboard 2

Cube 1

Page 88

Movie Matrix

M	U	N	C	H
M	O	T	H	S
H	A	V	O	C
A	T	T	I	C
G	L	A	R	E

ANSWERS

Monster Spotter's Guide

V I L E   FO U L E   E V IL

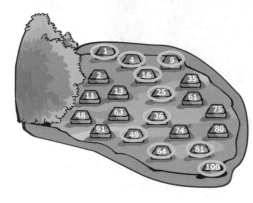

N I CE   I C K Y

Storyboard 3
Each time period is 10 minutes shorter than the one before. The next change is at 9.35, the fourth clock.

Page 89

Hop, Step, Jump
The path follows the squares of 1 to 10.

Sword in the Stone

Storyboard 4
SKELETON, SORCEROR, SQUIRREL, SMUGGLER and SCORPION.

Page 91

The Quest Begins

8 Turn Torah Swamp   **10** Point Ventric   **9** Black Mountain Castle   **5** Dors Saran Waterfall

2 Mannitol Plains   **4** The Greater Wall   **1** Vitriaco Forest   **3** Dors Saran Cliffs

6 Turbanssy Caves   **7** The Oamn't River   **11** The Oamn't Highway   **12** Lake Oamn't

On the Road Again
1. The road heads up a steep cliff.
2. The right. There's more trees.
3. The Wizard's Tower.
4. SW with the river current flowing out towards the sea.
5. He can't see Ventric Castle from the hut and Andoke Castle is too low. The light must have come from Black Mountain Castle.
6. On the beach near Point Ventric.
7. There are guard posts on the southern road.
8. South. If their feet are wet, they must be in the swamp.

Page 92

What's My Job?
SCRIPTWRITER

Screenplay
1. EXT: External 2. INT: Internal 3. O.S.: Off Screen
4. V.O.: Voice Over 5. CUT TO 6. FADE IN

Page 93

Storyboard 5
The knotted rope is a right-angled triangle with sides of 3, 4 and 5. If the rope was made as large as the dimensions in the diagram (which would need a lot of rope) it would be 50 times larger. The short side (the height of the cliff) would be 150 m.

ANSWERS

Across the Moat

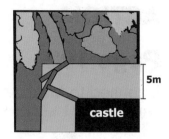

5m

castle

Storyboard 6
Read the dark brown stones first. Then read the gold coloured stones. Finally read the light coloured stones.

The inscription says: THIS DOOR IS LOCKED.

Page 94

Hollywood Crossquiz
HOOVES, OVERTOOK, LAGOON, LOOKALIKE, YEARBOOK, WOODWIND, ORDERBOOK, OVERCOOK, DOOM

What's Next?
The letter N. The puzzle spells out J R R TOLKIEN.

Storyboard 7
Each row, column and diagonal adds up to 34.

Page 95

Mirror, Mirror on the Wall

Storyboard 8
The teapot is in the tower marked 3. If you chose Tower 3 then the answer is $2\frac{1}{6}$ (2.16666…)

Page 96

Sword Play

FOIBLE
RAPIER
FORTE
SABRE
BLADE
SCIMITAR
SWORD
POMMEL
GUARD
GLADIUS

Storyboard 9
1. HORNET 2. ANOTHER 3. SHORTEN
4. NORTHERN 5. SOUTHERN

Page 97

Teapot of Double
Teapot 3 is the double.

Song for A'sthma
1. DEAD 2. DEAD 3. BEEF 4. CAGE

Probably number 3 would appeal most to a hungry dragon!

Storyboard 10
Did you try more than one answer? If you did, you'd realise that all the answers show your number. Why? If you multiply 12,345,679 by 9 you get 111,111,111.

Page 98

Rotten Monsters
Hints:

Clue 1: Niff can't have had 365 baths and must have had at least 1 (when mum washed out his mouth). To have had more baths, Mal'Odour can't have had 0 or 1 bath.

Clue 2: What smell would be in a second-hand shoe shop?

Clue 3: Mal'Odour can't have had 365 baths. El Pongo can't have had 0 or 1 baths.

Solution:

STENCH smells of sneakers, is scared of deodorant and has never had a bath.

MAL'ODOUR smells of garbage, is scared of perfume and has had 2 baths.

EL PONGO smells of banana skins, is scared of the scrubbing brush and has had 365 baths.

NIFF smells of dirty socks, is scared of soap and has only ever had one bath.

ANSWERS

Page 99

The Great Elf Guard Trivia Quiz
All the answers are (a).

Page 100

Cinema General Knowledge

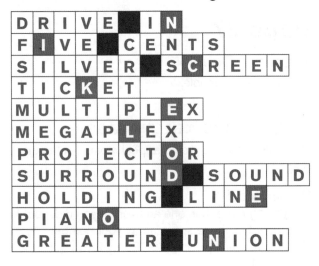

What's a Cinema?
The Greek word was 'Kinema'.

Page 101

Screen Aspect Ratios

1. 4 m wide
2. 4 m high
3. 10.6 m wide

2.35 into 1,33 doesn't go...
They all do! The three ways of fitting the widescreen picture onto your TV are:

1. cutting the sides off
2. creating black spaces at the top and bottom (letterbox)
3. squashing it sideways.

Watch out for all three styles on a TV near you.

ACTION

Page 102

Licensed to Make Money
THUNDERBALL was the highest grossing film.

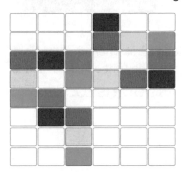

Page 103

Poster Posers
Anagrammaticals
1. SILENCER 2. MICRO DOT 3. DISGUISE
4. RENDEZVOUS

Quick Numbers
The Flavouring Daily puts out 365 issues (one each day), *The Washing Weekly* puts out 52 (one each week) and the *Ketchup Makers' Monthly* puts out 12 (one each month). 365 + 52 +12 = 429

Page 104

Synopsis Search
SHE WAS AN UNDERCOVER OPERATIVE

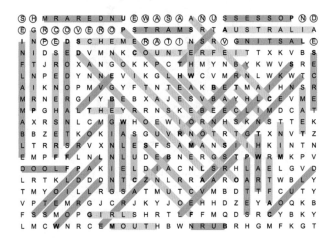

ANSWERS

Page 105

Beat the Bomb

Red Digits

1. Wonders of the ancient world 7
2. Signs of the zodiac 12
3. Cards in a deck (no jokers) 52
4. Known planets in the solar system 9
5. Squares on a chess board 64

Yellow Digits

1. Keys on a piano 88
2. Stars on the Australian flag 6
3. Holes on a golf course 18
4. A baker's dozen 13
5. Santa's reindeer (including Rudolph) 9

Blue Digits

1. Blind mice 3
2. Digits in an Australian postcode 4
3. Words a picture is worth 1000
4. Dalmatians 101
5. Days to travel around the world 80

The Final Time

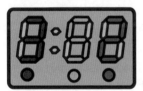

Storyboard 1
Rail car is the odd one out. All the others are palindromes and spell the same backwards and forwards.

Page 106

Jumbled Director
Robert RODRIGUEZ

Storyboard 2
SPY > POSY > SOPPY > SLOPPY

SPY > SPRY > SPRAY > PASTRY

Page 107

Target Practice

| BRANDY | 33 | RAY-SON | 31 | CINNA-MON | 39 | NUT-MEG | 40 |

Storyboard 3

B

Page 109

On Location

1. Mt Everest	Tibet	B
2. Stonehenge	United Kingdom	E
3. Dutch windmills	Netherlands	R
4. El Castillo	Mexico	M
5. Machu Pichu	Peru	U
6. Temple	Thailand	D
7. Niagara Falls	Canada	A
8. Venetian canals	Italy	T
9. Eiffel Tower	France	R
10. Taj Mahal	India	I
11. Statue of Liberty	USA	A
12. Samurai Castle	Japan	N
13. Greek ruins	Greece	G
14. Sydney Opera House	Australia	L
15. Egyptian Pyramid	Egypt	E

BERMUDA TRIANGLE

Fly the (Right) Flag
Flag 1 (Australia)

Why? The flags correspond to the countries in the centre column on page 108.

Odd one out
Group 1: Mt Everest – it's a natural landmark.

Group 2: A few possibilities. The Sydney Opera House because it's the only landmark not in Europe, or the Greek ruins because they are an ancient landmark.

ANSWERS

Page 110

Movie Matrix

M	A	G	I	C
C	O	A	S	T
C	I	V	I	L
S	H	E	I	K
F	A	L	S	E

Counterfeit Notes

1. The Reserve Bank isn't in Queensland.
2. Australia is not a republic.
3. It shows the Eiffel Tower.
4. It's signed by Ned Kelly.
5. And Blinky Bill.
6. The Australian flag is wrong.
7. It has a number 2.
8. It has the word 'four'.
9. It says one pound.
10. It features George Washington.

While we're at it, it's also the wrong colour and Australia doesn't produce one dollar notes any more!

Storyboard 4

Page 111

What's My Job?
DOLLY GRIP

What's Missing?
The missing letter is I.

Why? The letters spell out the name of the James Bond author IAN FLEMING.

Storyboard 5
2 Activate your personal warning system.
1 Be sure to first check the room is empty.
5 Extract the lamp's base and insert the bug.
6 Replace the base back onto the lamp.
4 Take out the lamp's plug from the power socket.
3 Then select a lamp in a suitable location.
7 You should finally check the bug is activated.

Page 112

Code Red (or Blue?)
Tea 4 Two
EUROPE

How? The letters are taken from the colours on each cup. Which letter? The number of spoons gives its position.

Speeding Fine
BYE BYE BETTY!

How? This time the speed sign gives us the message-letter's position in the alphabet.

Storyboard 6
ICE cream costs $2.00. Adding a D (ICED-cream) costs 50c more. DICED-cream has two Ds so it should cost $3.00.

RICE cream costs $3.00 so the R has added an extra $1.00 to the cost. CIDER-cream has an additional D and R over ICE-cream so it will cost $2.00 + $1.00 + 50c, or $3.50.

CRIER-cream has two extra Rs. Cost is $2.00 + $1.00 + $1.00: $4.00.

An easier way to work out the answer is to add 50c as you go down the price list.

Page 113

Calendar Code
This is very tricky (unless you guessed the holiday straight away, in which case you can work backwards to crack the code).

Did you notice that the dates have the numbers from 1–12? If you arrange them in order they look like this:

ANSWERS

Page 113 (cont)

Did you notice the same coloured pages have the same year? Or that the years have only three different ending numbers (1, 2 or 3)?

Did you happen to notice there are three letters in each month's name? If you happen to colour in the letter that matches the last digits of the year it looks like this:

Yes, it's the MELBOURNE CUP.

The extra points we mentioned? November 5, 2002.

Read 'Em and Weep

We mentioned scissors. If you cut the grid down the centre and swap the two halves over you get:

W	A	R	N	I	N	G	E
N	E	M	Y	O	P	E	R
A	T	I	V	E	S	H	A
V	E	D	I	S	C	O	V
E	R	E	D	T	H	E	K
E	Y	H	I	D	D	E	N
U	N	D	E	R	B	A	C
K	D	O	O	R	M	A	T

Which, if read continuously left to right (with some words split over two lines):

WARNING. ENEMY OPERATIVES HAVE DISCOVERED THE KEY HIDDEN UNDER BACKDOOR MAT

Page 114

Transmitter Trouble

This one's easier than it looks. Brandy's hint was 'how many sides does a triangle have? Then match the prongs' So let's include all the triangles with 3 prongs, all the squares with four and all the circles with one. Which leaves us with the exciting message:

TESTING 1 2 3

Storyboard 7

Silhouette 3 is the correct match. By the way, did you enjoy the 'pane-ful' pun?

Page 115

Hollywood Crossquiz

HILLSIDE, ODDBALL, LOLLIPOP, LAWFULLY YELLOW, WILLOW, OVERFULL, OFFICIALLY, DOLL

Storyboard 8

Cupboard 1 has green handles.

Cupboard 2 has three different books on its top shelf.

Cupboard 3 has an extra green book on the bottom shelf.

Cupboard 4 has a missing red book on the middle shelf.

Page 116

Cane Twisting

It can be twisted into 5 triangles.

Spot the Difference

TRACK (in the left sight) belongs in the right hand group. QUIET (on the right) belongs on the left.

Why?

All the words on the left are adjectives and the words on the right are verbs. (And yes quite a few on each side can be nouns as well but not enough to make it a solution.)

Storyboard 9

YELP has only one vowel in it. All the others have two.

ANSWERS

Page 117

I Spy

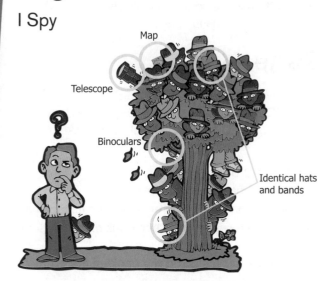

Map
Telescope
Binoculars
Identical hats and bands

How many spies altogether? If we're counting spy-heads and hats then 20 (and that's assuming the legs belong to the spy above them with the red hat). But someone appears to be looking through the telescope and someone else through the binoculars. So there's another two. And what about the guy in the blue shirt? Could he be a spy? And who's holding the map? Hey! Maybe the tree is a spy!

The answer then is 22… or 23… or maybe 25 or even 27…

Storyboard 10

Page 118

Information Update

Hints

Clue 1: The spy with the night vision goggles doesn't know karate.

Clue 2: What might a white Siamese cat be called? Pussikins perhaps?

Clue 3: What martial arts emphasises the use of hands?

Clue 4: What is the art of paper folding called?

Clue 5: What martial art might a Judogi be used in?

Clue 6: Careful—who likes to use the remote? Nut-Meg or Cinna-Mon?

Solution

NUT-MEG: Prefers karate, loves the TV remote and uses it to defeat her arch enemy Dr Yes.

BRANDY: Prefers judo and uses night goggles to capture her arch enemy XXL.

CINNA-MON: Prefers to use origami, loves her microwave and even offers the Count some hot popcorn from it when she defeats him.

RAY-SON: Likes to use Tae kwon do, loves his spy pen but is usually defeated by Pussikins, especially at tea-time.

Page 119

The Mint Spies: Afterburn Trivia Quiz

1. (b), **2.** (d), **3.** (c), **4.** (b), **5.** (b), **6.** (b), **7.** (a), **8.** (d), **9.** (d) – but only because he couldn't spell it, **10.** (a)